Second Edition
Skillful 1

CW00816057

Listening & Speaking Student's Book

Authors: Lida Baker and Steven Gershon
Series Consultant: Dorothy E. Zemach

SCOPE AND SEQUENCE

Grammar	Speaking	Study skills	Unit outcomes
Review and practice questions in the simple present	Notice and practice word stress in sentences Make formal and informal introductions Brainstorm and take part in an interview and introduce someone	Studying with others	Listen for key words to understand important information Listen for main ideas in the context of interviews and class discussions Ask and answer interview questions and introduce someone
Use adverbs of frequency to describe a routine	Recognize and use stress and intonation patterns in questions Practice getting attention and asking for permission Plan and conduct a survey about sleep habits	Strategies for taking notes while listening	Practice listening for specific information Listen for cause and effects Ask, answer, and discuss survey questions
Use comparative and superlative adjectives to compare types of university accommodation	Link consonants and vowels in connected speech Agree, disagree, and give an opinion Compare three types of university accommodation	Listening skills	Recognize and notice special terms to determine speaker attitude Predict the content of texts before listening Discuss, compare, and choose the best option
Use the present progressive to describe changes over time.	Pronounce contractions in the present progressive form Give clear reasons for or against an idea Plan, practice, and deliver a short talk about a trend in your city	Using information from lectures	Use interview questions to predict the contents of a talk Practice listening for advantages and disadvantages in the context of reports and podcasts Describe a trend in your city
Use modal verbs and adjective expressions to give advice	Notice and practice common syllable stress patterns in multi-syllable words Introduce your talk with signal terms and phrases Brainstorm, prepare, and present a short talk about a country's customs	Using slides in a presentation	Practice listening for explanations and examples in the context of a conversation Listen for the main ideas of a lecture to follow its organization Prepare and deliver a brief descriptive report

Grammar	Speaking	Study skills	Unit outcomes
Use the present passive to describe a process	Pronounce the past –ed ending of different words Use signal words and phrases to explain and define ideas Plan and describe the process of making a type of food	Active and passive learning	Listen for facts and opinions Listen for steps in a process Plan, organize, and describe a process
Use can and be able to to express and talk about ability	Recognize and pronounce can, can't and be able to / not able to in affirmative, negative, and interrogative sentences Use words and phrases to give a description Take part in a memory quiz and give a description of an animal	How do you remember things?	Practice recognizing categories to better understand a description Listen for words used to classify items in the context of an interview Prepare and take part in a quiz about a discipline of science Give a description
Use gerunds and infinitives to give more information about a photograph	Identify, distinguish, and pronounce words beginning with /p/ and /b/ Use words and phrases to describe the location of items in a photograph Describe a photograph	Rounding up and down	Practice listening for numbers in the context of an interview Listen for descriptive details Describe a photograph
Use used to to talk about differences between past and present	Identify and pronounce stress for emphasis Use concluding words and phrases to end a presentation Brainstorm, plan, and deliver a short talk on how life has changed in the last ten years	Using technology to personalize learning	Follow a sequence in a conversation by listening for past and present time signals Listen and identify concluding phrases in a presentation Describe differences between the past and the present
Use will to make predictions about the future	Pronounce contractions with will Use future time markers to talk about future developments and trends Give a short presentation about work in the future	Combining work and study	Listen for words and phrases that signal additional information Listen for the overall structure of a talk or lecture Plan and deliver a short presentation

To the student

Academic success requires so much more than memorizing facts. It takes skills. This means that a successful student can both learn and think critically.

Skillful gives you:

- Skills you need to succeed when reading and listening to academic texts
- Skills you need to succeed when writing for and speaking to different audiences
- Skills for critically examining the issues presented by a speaker or a writer
- Study skills for learning and remembering the English language and important information.

To successfully use this book, use these strategies:

Come to class prepared to learn. This means that you should show up well fed, well rested, and prepared with the proper materials. Watch the video online and look at the discussion point before starting each new unit.

Ask questions and interact. Learning a language is not passive. You need to actively participate. Help your classmates, and let them help you. It is easier to learn a language with other people.

Practice! Memorize and use new language. Use the *Skillful* online practice to develop the skills presented in the Student's Book. Revise vocabulary on the review page.

Review your work. Look over the skills, grammar, and vocabulary from previous units. Study a little bit each day, not just before tests.

Be an independent learner, too. Look for opportunities to study and practice English outside of class, such as reading for pleasure and using the Internet in English. Remember that learning skills, like learning a language, takes time and practice. Be patient with yourself, but do not forget to set goals. Check your progress and be proud of your success! I hope you enjoy using *Skillful*!

Dorothy E. Zemach – Series Consultant

Opening page

Each unit starts with two opening pages. These pages get you ready to study the topic of the unit. There is a video to watch and activities to do before you start your class.

Listening lessons

In every unit, there are two listening lessons and they present two different aspects of the unit topic and help you with ideas and language for your speaking task

Vocabulary to prepare you for the listening activities

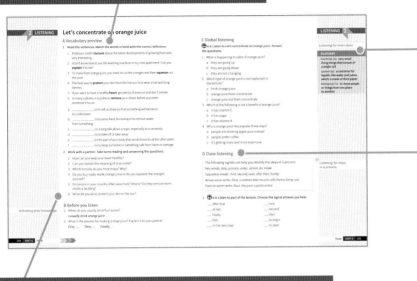

Glossaries help you understand higher level words from the listening text.

Every listening section helps you use a new listening skill.

Develop your listening skills in each part of the listening lesson.

Speaking lessons

After your listening lessons, there is a page for you to analyze a model answer to a speaking task. This will help you organize your ideas and language and prepare for your final task at the end of the unit.

First analyze the model answer.

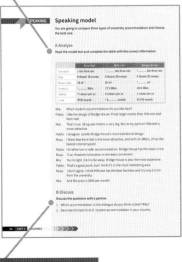

Brainstorm your speaking task and organize your ideas and language from the unit.

Finally, perform your speaking task.

Next, discuss your ideas.

The Birth Order Effect

TOP CAREERS FOR FIRST-BORNS

 Government

 Information Technology

 Company boss

Science

TOP CAREERS FOR MIDDLE CHILDREN

 Public Service

 Construction

 Teacher

 Police

TOP CAREERS FOR YOUNGEST CHILDREN

 Design/Art

 Sales

 Editing and Writing

 Sports coach

TOP CAREERS FOR ONLY CHILDREN

 Business person

 Information Technology

Nursing

 Engineering

Discussion point

Discuss with a partner.

1 How many brothers and sisters do you have? Are you a first-born, middle, last-born, or only child?

2 What job would you like to have in the future?

3 Does the infographic match the job you want?

4 Think about your family. Is the information in the infographic correct?

100% ASTRONAUTS WHO'VE GONE INTO SPACE WERE EITHER FIRST-BORN CHILDREN OR FIRST-BORN SONS

VIDEO

ANIMAL PERSONALITY

Before you watch

Match the words in bold with the correct definition.

1 **interesting** (adj)   a to find an answer to a problem

2 **solve** (v)   b a group of people, animals, or things

3 **test** (v)   c not boring

4 **type** (n)   d to find out if something works

UNIT AIMS

LISTENING 1 Listening for key words
LISTENING 2 Listening for main ideas
STUDY SKILL Studying with others

VOCABULARY Words to describe personality
GRAMMAR Simple present questions
SPEAKING Making introductions

A first-born child.

While you watch

Watch the video. Answer the questions.

1 Where was the experiment?

   a Outside, in a forest   b In a room, in a university

2 Where did gray squirrels that now live in the UK come from?

   a England   b North America

3 What did the scientists in the study watch the squirrels do?

   a Solve problems   b Live in a tree

4 What are the gray squirrels good at finding?

   a Food   b Other squirrels

After you watch

Discuss the questions with your partner.

1 What is your favorite animal?

   My favorite animal is …

2 Do you like watching animal documentaries?

   Yes, I like watching animal documentaries because …

3 Is it important to study animals?

   Yes, it is very important because …

   No, I don't think it is important because …

First day on campus

A Vocabulary preview

1 Match the words in bold with the correct definition.

1	**birth order** (n)	a	the way you think, feel, and behave; your personality
2	**character** (n)	b	relaxed, calm
3	**describe** (v)	c	when you were born compared to your brothers and sisters
4	**easy-going** (adj)		
5	**research** (n)	d	to give details about what someone or something is like
6	**serious** (adj)	e	something that you learn or teach in school, e.g. mathematics
7	**strict** (adj)	f	carefully following the rules for correct behavior or action
8	**subject** (n)	g	a detailed study of a subject to discover new information
		h	someone who thinks carefully about things and doesn't laugh much

2 Complete the sentences with the words in bold from Exercise 1.

1 I think my _____ is more like my mother's than my father's.

2 I can _____ my father as serious and strict, but also kind.

3 I like people who are _____, cheerful, and happy.

4 I'm very different from my friend even though our _____ is the same in our families.

5 It's difficult to make me laugh because I'm a _____ person.

6 My best _____ this semester is English.

7 I would like to do a _____ project about birth order before I graduate from college.

8 I think it's better to have a _____ teacher who makes us follow the rules.

3 Work with a partner. Which sentences in Exercise 2 are true for you?

B Before you listen

Activating prior knowledge

Discuss with a partner.

1 Which subjects in school are you most interested in? Which ones are difficult for you?

I'm most interested in … I think the most difficult subjects are …

2 Do you sometimes visit your teachers or professors in their office? What do you talk about?

I often / sometimes / don't visit … We talk about …

C Global listening

The key words and phrases in a conversation give you important information about the topics the speakers are talking about, and also some of the details. The key words are often:

- nouns: *classes, professor, campus*
- verbs: *introduce, teach, ask*
- adjectives: *friendly, creative, younger*

Listening for key words

 **1.1** Listen to two people talking at Central University. Choose the best answer to complete each sentence.

1 Nina and Dilara are …
  a professors.
  b students.
  c co-workers.

2 Dilara and Nina talk to the professors …
  a in Nina's classroom.
  b in the library.
  c in the professors' offices.

3 Dilara and Nina talk to …
  a two professors.
  b three professors.
  c four professors.

4 Dr. Sperling asks Dilara questions …
  a because Dilara wants to take her class.
  b to check Dilara's class work.
  c for her research.

5 Dr. Sperling asks Dilara about …
  a her family and character.
  b her classes and teachers.
  c her hobbies and subjects.

Taking notes while listening

D Close listening

1 🎧 **1.2** Listen again to the first part of the conversation. Read Dilara's notes and choose the correct option.

> Prof. Malik's office: ¹**6D / 6B**
> Course: ²**English Literature /**
> **English Language**
> ³**Friendly / Unfriendly**, easy-going,
> not too serious
> *Can answer lots of questions
>
> Dr. Sperling's office: ⁴**16D / 6D**
> Course: ⁵**Biology / Psychology**
> Great teacher: open-minded, creative,
> but strict
> `⁶**Likes to ask questions / Doesn't like**
> **to ask questions**

2 🎧 **1.3** Listen to Dr. Sperling's interview with Dilara. Complete her notes with no more than one word or a number.

> Name: Dilara
>
> From: Ankara, Turkey
>
> Family: ¹_____ brother(s) _____ sister(s)
>
> Birth order: ²_____
>
> Personality: reliable, hard-working, ³_____
>
> Future job: ⁴_____

E Critical thinking

Discuss the questions.

1 Which professor would you prefer to have for a class, Professor Malik or Dr. Sperling? Why?

I would prefer to have … because he/she …

2 Do you think Dilara's character will help her be a good teacher? Why?

I think Dilara would/wouldn't be a good teacher because she is/isn't …

3 Do you agree with this quote about teachers?

A teacher's personality is more important than the subject they teach.

I agree/disagree with this quote because …

Pronunciation for listening

Reduced final /t/ before a consonant

In spoken English, when a word ends with /t/, it is not always fully pronounced if the following word begins with a consonant.

Here are some examples from *First day on campus*:

What job do you want?   *She's a great teacher.*   *Are you the oldest child?*

1   🎧 1.4 Underline the words with the final /t/ before a word which begins with a consonant sound. Listen and notice that the final /t/ is not fully pronounced.

   1   I'm the youngest child in my family.

   2   It's my first day in college.

   3   I want to be a doctor in the future.

   4   I have an important class in the morning.

   5   What subject do you study?

2   🎧 1.5 Listen to these sentences from *First day on campus*. Write the missing word you hear.

   1   Really? _____ would be great.

   2   How is your _____ day on campus?

   3   I'd like you to _____ Dilara.

   4   Well, I _____ to be a teacher.

   5   It's all _____ your birth order in the family.

3   Read the sentences in Exercise 2 with a partner. Use the reduced /t/ sound.

She's a great teacher.

2 LISTENING

Birth order and personality

A Vocabulary preview

1 Match the words in bold with the correct definition.

   1 When there is a problem at home, I **usually** try to solve it.

   2 I must work hard to get **attention** in my family.

   3 I'm not very **comfortable** around loud people as I'm a quiet person.

   4 I don't think birth order has a big **effect** on my personality.

   a feeling relaxed or calm around other people

   b the result of an action or change

   c the thought or interest you give to or receive from someone

   d generally, normally

   5 My friends think I'm **funny**. They always laugh at my jokes.

   6 I'm very **organized** and so I like to plan as much as I can.

   7 I am a very **social** person so I often go out and see my friends.

   8 I love to speak about a lot of things with my friends; I'm very **talkative**.

   e someone who likes to speak a lot

   f someone or something that makes people laugh or smile

   g someone who can plan their work, studies or life well

   h someone who enjoys being with other people

2 Work with a partner. Which sentences (1–8) in Exercise 1 are true for you?

B Before you listen

Activating prior knowledge

1 Look at the picture and write the words below next to each child.

> First-born   Middle child   Last-born

2 Choose two words that describe your personality.
Discuss with a partner and give examples.

> easy-going funny organized
> social serious strict talkative

C Global listening

Listening for main ideas

The main idea is the most important idea in a listening passage. A short passage might have one main idea. To identify the main ideas, ask yourself: "What are the most important ideas in the passage?"

Words and phrases that often signal a main idea include:
- phrases like *to begin, let's start, next, and finally*
- questions like *what is…, why is…, and what about …*

🔊 1.6 Read the topics from *Birth order and personality* below. Then listen and put the main ideas in the order you hear them.

___ A First-born children   ___ D Last-born children

___ B Only children   ___ E Why is birth order important?

_1_ C What is birth order?   ___ F Middle children

Listening for main ideas

D Close listening

1 🎧 **1.6** Read the main ideas from *Birth order and personality*. Notice the key words in bold. Choose *T* (True) or *F* (False) for each sentence.

1 Birth order has a **small** effect on our personality. T / F

2 First born children are **serious**, responsible and organized. T / F

3 Middle children are **social** and their friends are important to them. T / F

4 Last-born children **always** get lots of attention. T / F

5 Only children are **not** comfortable around adults. T / F

2 🎧 **1.7** Listen to part of the interview. Match the birth order with the correct personality adjectives.

1 First-born children are   a friendly

2 Middle children are   b talkative

3 Last-born children are   c natural leaders

4 Only children are   d sweet and loving

E Critical thinking

Discuss the questions.

1 Interview a partner. Complete the first three rows with your partner's information. Look again at your answers in Part D and complete row 4 with the correct personality adjectives.

1 How many brothers and / or sisters do you have? How old are they?	
2 What is your birth order in your family?	
3 How would you describe your personality?	
4 Typical personality for this birth order	
5 Is there a difference between row 3 and row 4?	

2 Think of your own family or a family you know well. Is the information about first-born, middle, last-born, and only children correct or incorrect?

I think the information is correct/incorrect because …

3 Look back at your answers in Exercise 1. Does birth order affect your partner's personality?

My partner is …, so I think birth order does/doesn't …

Study skills   Studying with others

You might do some academic tasks with other students which need skills such as:

- Taking an active part, without talking too much or without other students making all the decisions.
- Working together in a team or group, face-to-face, and/or using video links or social networking.
- Supporting others, encouraging them, and sharing ideas.

© Stella Cottrell (2013)

1   Make a list of three personality characteristics you need to work with others.

2   Compare your list with a partner.

To work with others, I think we need to be …   *What do you think?*

3   Which characteristics do you have? Which characteristics do you need to improve?

I think I am …   *However, I'd like to be more …*

Vocabulary development

Words to describe personality

1 Read the sentences. Complete the definitions below using a word in bold from the sentences.

1 My aunt is very **generous**. She sends me a card and a big present for my birthday every year. She's also very **polite**. She always says "*please*" and "*thank you.*"

2 My brother spends most of the day sitting on the sofa and watching TV. He's so **lazy**! However, he always gets excellent grades at school. I don't know how he does it. He must be very **intelligent**.

3 I get really **shy** when I meet new people and I don't talk a lot to them. I want to improve this because it's important to be **confident** and believe in yourself more.

4 My friend takes fantastic photographs. He is really **creative** and always has lots of new ideas for pictures. The problem is that he is quite **selfish**. He doesn't like to share his ideas or help other people.

a _____ people believe in their own ability to be successful.

b A _____ person doesn't like to do any activity that needs effort.

c _____ people are smart and usually do well in school.

d A _____ person does not talk about how they feel.

e A _____ person only thinks about themselves.

f _____ people help others, often by giving their time or money.

g A _____ person gives their time or money to other people.

h _____ people have lots of new ideas.

2 Choose the best personality adjective from Exercise 1 for each description.

> **1** I have a new lab partner, David, who is social and friendly. The problem is that he doesn't work hard at all. It is very difficult because I need to write a lot of work for him.
> _____

> **2** My friend, Marta, is an artist. She paints pictures of cities in the morning and they're really beautiful. I have two of her paintings in my living room. She always has lots of new ideas.
> _____

> **3** My classmate, Sophie, is really smart. She always gets the best grades in class and she works really hard. She knows lots of information about different subjects, including the subjects she doesn't study!
> _____

3 Do you know anyone like David, Marta, or Sophie? Describe them to a partner.

Yes, my brother is very …

Academic words

1 Match the words in bold with the correct definition.

1	**goals** (n)	a	to think that something is true
2	**grades** (n)	b	work that you do regularly to earn money
3	**job** (n)	c	things that you hope to achieve in the future
4	**positive** (adj)	d	anything that is bad, not wanted, not helpful
5	**negative** (adj)	e	a letter or number that shows the quality of a student's work
6	**believe** (v)	f	anything that is good, wanted, and helpful

2 Complete each sentence with a word in bold from Exercise 1.

1 Does your personality help you to be a successful student who gets good _____?

2 Do you _____ that culture and gender have a big effect on your personality?

3 What are your career _____ for the future?

4 Would you like to change any _____ characteristics that you don't like about yourself?

5 What is one _____ characteristic that you would like to have?

6 In your country, do people ask about your personality at a _____ interview?

3 Answer the questions in Exercise 2 and explain your answers to a partner.

I think my personality helps / doesn't help me be a successful student because I'm …

Speaking model

You are going to learn how to ask questions in the simple present tense, make introductions, and pronounce sentence stress. You are then going to use the questions to interview someone and introduce him or her to others.

A Analyze

1 🎧 1.8 Complete the conversation below with the correct questions from the box. Then listen and check your answers.

> What are three words that describe your character?   Where are you from?
> What job do you want to have in the future?   Are you the oldest?
> Do you have any brothers and sisters?

Yakub

Jay: What's your name?

Yakub: Yakub Mara.

Jay: ¹_____?

Yakub: I'm from Jordan.

Jay: ²_____?

Yakub: Yes, I have one brother and two sisters.

Jay: ³_____?

Yakub: No, I'm the second oldest.

Jay: ⁴_____?

Yakub: I'm serious, responsible, and organized.

Jay: ⁵_____?

Yakub: I want to be a doctor.

2 Complete Jay's introduction of Yakub with the words from the box.

> middle   pleasure   responsible   first   children

Hi everybody. It's my ¹_____ to introduce Yakub Mara to you. He's from Jordan. There are four ²_____ in Yakub's family, and he's the second oldest. But his personality is not like a ³_____ child. I think his personality is like a ⁴_____-born child because he is serious, ⁵_____ and organized. He wants to be a doctor when he graduates.

B Discuss

1 What other personality characteristics does a doctor need?

   I think doctors should also be …

2 What other jobs fit Yakub's personality?

   I think other jobs that fit Yakub's personality are …

Grammar

Simple present tense questions

Form	Example
Yes/no questions	
Is/Are + subject Do/Does + subject + verb (base form)	*Is the teacher strict?* *(Yes, he is. / No, she isn't.)* *Are they brothers?* *(Yes, they are. / No, they aren't.)* *Does your sister enjoy sports?* *(Yes, she does. / No, she doesn't.)* *Do your brothers go to the same school?* *(Yes, they do. / No, they don't.)*
Wh- questions	
Wh- + is/are Wh- + do/does + subject + verb (base form)	*What is the baby's name? (Joseph.)* *Who are your parents? (Mr. and Mrs. Enani.)* *What do you want to do when you graduate?* *(I want to be a doctor.)* *Where does your mother work?* *(At a school.)*

1 Rearrange the words to form questions. Then ask and answer the questions with a partner.

you / only child / are / an   *Are you an only child?*

Yes, I am an only child   *No, I'm not an only child.*

1 have / do / brothers / you / sisters / and / any   _____?
2 good / you / student / a / are   _____?
3 your / strict / teacher / is / English   _____?
4 person / you / are / funny / a   _____?
5 enjoy / studies / your / do / you   _____?
6 a / talkative / are / person / you   _____?

2 Complete the wh- questions with the correct form of be or do. Then ask and answer the questions with a partner.

Where _____ you from?   *Where are you from?*   *I am from Dubai.*

1 What _____ your full name?   _____.
2 Where _____ your family live?   _____.
3 What _____ your hobbies?   _____.
4 When _____ your birthday?   _____.
5 Who _____ your best friends?   _____.
6 What job _____ you want to have in the future?   _____.

Speaking skill

English has many expressions for introducing people to each other. Some expressions are informal and some are formal. We often use informal phrases with friends, classmates, and people we know well. We often use formal phrases with teachers, family, and people in high positions.

Abdullah, this is my friend, Carlos. informal

I'd like you to meet my classmate, Sonya.

I'd like to introduce my teacher, Mrs. Kim

It is my pleasure to introduce our director, Mr. Smith. formal

1 Complete the introductions with expressions from the skills box above.

1 Hi Nasrin, I'd _____ meet my colleague, Soo-Mi.

2 Richard, I'd _____ introduce my grandfather, Mr. Garcia.

3 Hi Ali. I'd like you _____ my brother, Sami.

4 Hello class. It's my _____ introduce our Dean, Mr. Dalman.

5 Paul, _____ my friend, Miko.

2 Role-play in a group of three. Read the situations below. Take turns introducing your partners to each other. Use the expressions from the box that match the person you are introducing.

Possible situations

1 Your father to your teacher.

2 The director of your company to a visitor from Japan.

3 Your best friend to a new classmate.

4 Your brother to a work colleague.

5 Your uncle to your neighbor.

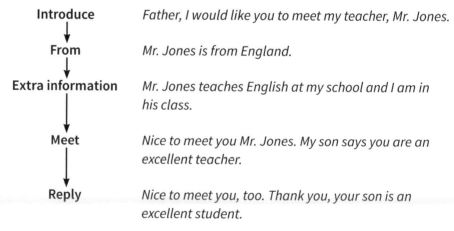

Introduce	*Father, I would like you to meet my teacher, Mr. Jones.*
From	*Mr. Jones is from England.*
Extra information	*Mr. Jones teaches English at my school and I am in his class.*
Meet	*Nice to meet you Mr. Jones. My son says you are an excellent teacher.*
Reply	*Nice to meet you, too. Thank you, your son is an excellent student.*

Pronunciation for speaking

Word stress in sentences

The important words in a sentence are stressed. This means they sound higher, louder, and clearer than the unstressed words in the sentence. A speaker can choose to stress any important words in a sentence.

Words that are normally stressed:

nouns, verbs (except *be*), adjectives, some adverbs, negative words, and *Wh-* question words.

Words that are normally unstressed:

auxiliary verbs, pronouns, articles, and prepositions.

Do you <u>have</u> any <u>brothers</u> and <u>sisters</u>?

Are you a <u>serious person</u>?

<u>Where</u> were you <u>born</u>?

1 🎧 **1.9 Listen and notice the stressed words. Then listen again and repeat.**

   1 I can <u>introduce</u> you to some <u>professors now</u>.
   2 My <u>brother</u> and <u>sister</u> are <u>younger</u> than me.
   3 She's a <u>great teacher</u>, very <u>open-minded</u> and <u>creative</u>, but <u>strict</u>.
   4 <u>Birth order means</u> your <u>place</u> or your <u>position</u> in the <u>family</u>.
   5 <u>Why</u> is <u>birth order important</u>?
   6 <u>Last-born children</u> are very <u>sweet</u> and <u>loving</u>.

2 🎧 **1.8 Underline the words you think are stressed. Then listen and check your answers.**

   Jay: What's your name?
   Yakub: Yakub Mara.
   Jay: Where are you from?
   Yakub: I'm from Jordan.
   Jay: Do you have any brothers and sisters?
   Yakub: Yes, I have one brother and two sisters.
   Jay: Are you the oldest?
   Yakub: No, I'm the second oldest.
   Jay: What are three words that describe your character?
   Yakub: I'm serious, responsible, and organized.
   Jay: What job do you want to have in the future?
   Yakub: I want to be a doctor.

3 Read the interview with a partner. Focus on your word stress.

Speaking task

Interview someone and introduce him or her to the class. You must speak for at least 30 seconds.

Brainstorm

Complete the word map with two extra topics you can ask your partner about.

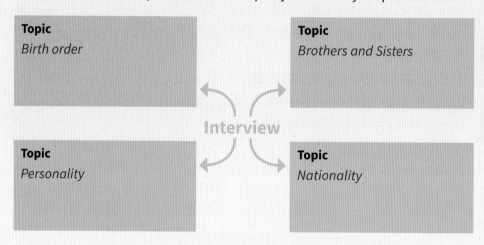

Topic
Birth order

Topic
Brothers and Sisters

Interview

Topic
Personality

Topic
Nationality

Plan

Look back at your word map. Write five questions to ask someone. Use the grammar box on page 21 and the vocabulary from this unit to help you.

Speak

Ask and answer your questions with a partner. Take notes on your partner's answers.

Share

Form a group. Introduce your partner to the other students. Use expressions for making an introduction on page 22 and remember to stress important words. Make notes about your group members' answers.

Reflect

Read the question.

Does birth order affect your personality?

Choose the answer that matches your opinion. Explain why.

| Yes, a lot | Yes, a little | No, not very much | No, not at all |

Is your opinion similar or different from your classmates?

Review

Wordlist

MACMILLAN
DICTIONARY

Vocabulary preview

attention (n) ***	effect (n) ***	strict (adj) **
birth order (n)	funny (adj) ***	subject (n) ***
character (n) ***	organized (adj) ***	talkative (adj) ***
comfortable (adj) ***	research (n) ***	usually (adv)***
describe (v) ***	serious (adj) ***	
easy-going (adj)	social (adj) ***	

Vocabulary development

confident (adj) **	intelligent (adj) **	selfish (adj) *
creative (adj) **	lazy (adj) **	shy (adj)*
generous (adj) **	polite (adj) *	

Academic words

believe (v) ***	grades (n)**	negative (adj) ***
goals (n) **	job (n)***	positive (adj) ***

Academic words review

Complete the sentences with the words in the box.

believe	goals	grades	job	negative

1 I _____ that birth order affects a person's personality.
2 I would like to have a _____ in design or engineering in the future.
3 You need to get good _____ at university to get a good job.
4 _____ characteristics, like being selfish and lazy, are not good when working in a team.
5 My _____ this year are to pass my exams and learn a language.

Unit review

Listening 1		I can listen for key words.
Listening 2		I can listen for the main ideas of a topic.
Vocabulary		I can use vocabulary to talk about personality.
Grammar		I can use simple present tense questions.
Speaking skill		I can make introductions.
Pronunciation		I can pronounce word stress in sentences.

ARE YOU A "DAY PERSON" OR A "NIGHT PERSON"?

Discussion point

Study the infographic and answer the questions.

1 Who gets more sleep, day people or night people?

2 Are night people older or younger?

3 Who gets jet lag going east?

4 Based on the information, are you a day person or a night person?

	Day people	Night people
Time	late morning	late afternoon, evening
Alarm clock	not necessary	necessary
Feeling in the morning	happy, full of energy	tired
Feeling at night	tired	happy, full of energy
Travel	gets jet lag going west	gets jet lag going east
Age	many people over 60	teens and young adults
Amount of sleep	enough	often not enough

VIDEO

SLEEP BREAK

Before you watch

Work with your partner. Discuss these questions.

1 How do you relax after a busy day?

2 What time of day do you usually feel tired?

3 When you are tired, what do you do to give you energy?

UNIT AIMS

LISTENING 1 Listening for specific information
LISTENING 2 Listening for effects
STUDY SKILL Strategies for taking notes while listening

VOCABULARY Words to describe waking and sleeping
GRAMMAR Adverbs of frequency
SPEAKING Getting attention and asking for permission

Children at sunset in India.

While you watch

Watch the video. Answer the questions.

1 Which city are the sleeping pods in?
   a   Los Angeles   b   New York
2 When does the sleeping pod wake you up?
   a   after 20 minutes   b   after 30 minutes
3 Why does the writer, Ben, use the sleeping pod?
   a   he drinks too much coffee   b   it gives him energy
4 What does the businessman, Ed, do in the pod?
   a   sleep   b   think and be creative

After you watch

Work with a partner. Discuss the questions.

1 Do you think sleeping pods are a good idea? Why? / Why not?
   I think it's a good/bad idea because …
2 What is the best time of day to use a sleeping pod?
   I think … is the best time of day to use a sleeping pod.
3 Where is a good place to put sleeping pods?
   A good place to put sleeping pods is …

The clock in our brain

A Vocabulary preview

1 Match the words in bold with the correct definition.

1	**active** (adj)	a	when something repeats in the same order
2	**awake** (adj)	b	the part of the body we use for thinking and feeling
3	**brain** (n)	c	not sleeping
4	**cycle** (n)	d	busy; doing a lot of different activities
5	**daily** (adj)	e	to discover or learn
6	**expect** (v)	f	usual
7	**find out** (v)	g	happening every day
8	**regular** (adj)	h	to think or believe something will happen

2 Complete the sentences with the words in bold from Exercise 1.

1 I believe that learning a new language makes my _____ stronger.

2 When I need to study at night and feel tired, I drink coffee or energy drinks to stay _____.

3 I am a "morning person". I am most _____ early in the morning, and I don't have much energy in the evening.

4 I sometimes get into a bad sleep _____ when I go to bed late too many times in one week.

5 I _____ to finish school and start working in four years.

6 Vegetables are a _____ part of my diet. I eat them at almost every meal.

7 Exercise is an important part of my _____ routine. I run every day before breakfast.

8 I use social media to _____ what is happening in the world.

3 Work with a partner. Which sentences in Exercise 2 are true for you?

B Before you listen

Activating prior knowledge

1 Look at the list of activities. When do you usually do them? Discuss with a partner.

I usually eat breakfast at 7:30 in the morning.

wake up	start class
exercise	study
eat breakfast, lunch, and dinner	watch a movie
meet friends	go to bed

2 How do you feel if you do the activities above at a different time?

C Global listening

🎧 **2.1** Listen to *The clock in our brain*. Choose the best answer to complete each sentence.

Listening for main ideas

1 The conversation is about …
   a jet lag.
   b people's body clock.
   c people who work at night.

2 Circadian rhythm responds to …
   a temperature.
   b exercise.
   c light.

3 Scientists studied what happened when people …
   a didn't know the time or see daylight.
   b worked all the time.
   c didn't have a 24-hour clock.

4 Jet lag happens when people …
   a don't sleep enough.
   b spend time outside.
   c fly long distances.

5 If you have jet lag, you should …
   a go outside in the morning.
   b go to bed early.
   c take medicine.

GLOSSARY

adjust (v) to change something to make it more accurate

circadian rhythm (n) the changes in people's brains that happen in 24 hours (the body clock)

jet lag (n) the feeling of being very tired and sometimes confused because you have flown quickly across parts of the world where the time is different

volunteer (n) someone who helps scientists in a study, or works for no money

D Close listening

Listening for specific information

> Specific information means facts and details that speakers give to support a main idea. To recognize specific information, listen closely for:
> - names of people, places, or things
> - dates, numbers, and definitions.

1 Read the sentences below. Think about what information from the skills box you will hear.

1 The study on circadian rhythm happened for two months in the ____1970s____.

2 'Volunteers' means the people who helped in the _____.

3 The volunteers were in a _____ with no windows or clocks.

4 The scientists expected the _____ to have an exact 24-hour cycle.

5 They discovered that 75% of people actually have a 24.2 or _____ and a half hour cycle.

2 🎧 2.2 Listen again to part of the interview. Complete the sentences in Exercise 1 with one word or a number.

3 🎧 2.3 Listen to the second part of the interview. Correct the mistakes in bold in each sentence.

1 Jet lag happens when people **drive** long distances East or West.

2 Jet lag makes people feel **sleepy** at night.

3 New York and Beijing have a **14**-hour time difference.

4 When we travel, **food** helps our brain adjust to the difference in time.

E Critical thinking

Discuss the questions.

1 Would you like a job that needs you to be awake at night? Why or why not?

I would/wouldn't like a job that needs me to be awake at night because …

2 What things in the box can make people tired?

| diet | exercise | health | routine | weather | work |

People can also get tired when …

3 Do you think information about circadian rhythm is helpful? Why?

I think information about circadian rhythm is/isn't helpful because …

Study skills — Strategies for taking notes while listening

1 Write key words and main ideas.
2 Write phrases, not full sentences.
3 Use abbreviations.
4 Use headings.
5 Indent details under headings.
6 Use symbols instead of words.
7 Number the points in each part.

© Stella Cottrell (2013)

1 Look at the notes for part of *The clock in our brain* below. Write the words in the box in the correct places next to the notes.

abbreviation   heading   numbers   symbol   indent

Circadian rhythm ➝ 1 _____

1. = parts of brain that control activities like eating, sleeping

2. responds to light & dark   2 _____   3 _____

Studies in 1960s–1970s

1. Sci. wanted to know: When do people fall asleep if they don't

know what time it is?

2. Put volun. in room w/out windows for 2 mos.

3. Found: 75% of volun. had daily cycle 24.2 – 24.5 hrs

4 _____   5 _____

2 Work with a partner. Look at the notes again and find more examples of each strategy in the study skills box.

3 Look again at the strategies for taking notes while listening. Which strategies do you use? Which strategies are most useful, in your opinion?

The strategies I use for taking notes are …
The strategies I find most useful are …

Time to sleep

A Vocabulary preview

1 Read these sentences. Match the words in bold with the correct definition.

   1 In the winter, bears sleep for a **period** of several months.

   2 In the U.S., it is **typical** for college students to live in a dormitory during their first year.

   3 My sleep **pattern** is always the same: I go to sleep at midnight and wake up at seven.

   4 Max spends a **total** of about 30 hours a week online.

   a _____ (n) the regular way that something happens

   b _____ (adj) common or usual

   c _____ (n) the number you get when you add all the other numbers

   d _____ (n) an amount of time

   5 Rana hates shopping in large stores because there are too many **choices**.

   6 Please don't **interrupt** me. Wait until I'm finished speaking.

   7 It is **natural** for babies to start smiling when they are 6 to 12 weeks old.

   8 Fish oil is a very **healthy** food. It helps the brain work better.

   e _____ (adj) good for the body

   f _____ (n) things you choose

   g _____ (adj) the usual way something happens

   h _____ (v) to stop something or someone before they finish

2 Discuss the questions with a partner.

1 Is it typical for students to live in a dormitory during the first year of university in your country, or do they live at home?

   It is/isn't typical for students in my country to live …

2 How many hours do you spend online in total each week?

   I spend a total of … hours online each week.

3 What healthy food do you eat? *I eat …*

B Before you listen

Activating prior knowledge

Work with a partner. Ask and answer the questions. Then find another classmate. Tell him or her about your first partner.

1 How many hours do you usually sleep at one time?

2 Do you wake up during the night?

3 Do you ever take a nap during the day?

   I talked to Gina. She usually … She doesn't … She never ….

C Global listening

1 🎧 **2.4** Listen to *Time to sleep*. Match the items to make true statements.

Listening for main ideas

1	The lecture	a	is not healthy.
2	Monophasic sleep	b	refers to two sleep periods per day.
3	Biphasic sleep	c	is about three sleep patterns.
4	Multiphasic sleep	d	is typical for most people.

2 Match the three different types of sleep patterns in the box with the diagrams.

Biphasic   Monophasic   Multiphasic

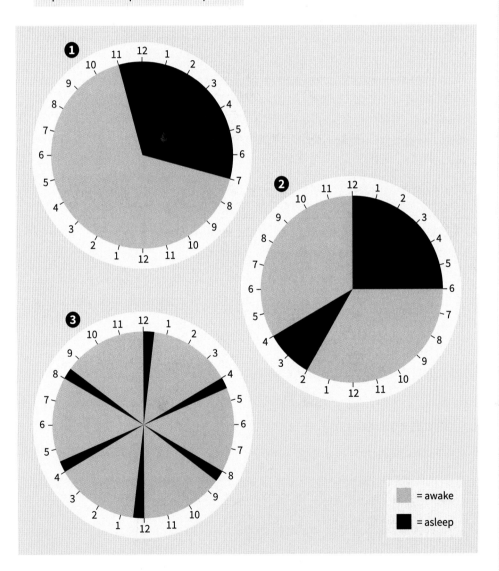

= awake

= asleep

D Close listening

1 🎧 2.5 Listen to the first part of the lecture again. Correct the four mistakes in the notes.

Monophasic cycle (Mono = 2)
    Ppl sleep 6–8 hours in 1 period of time, awake 6–18 hours
Biphasic cycle (Bi = 2)
    2x sleeps = Sweden
    Sleep 5–6 hrs @ night + nap in afternoon

Listening for effects

> A result, or *effect*, is what happens because of a cause. To recognize effects, listen for these signals: *As a result, so, this means*.
>
> Mika drinks coffee at 10 p.m. <u>As a result</u>, she is awake most of the night. My sister and I are "night people," <u>so</u> we often talk on the phone after 1 a.m.
>
> When you take notes, you can use an arrow to show the relationship between causes and effects.
>
> **cause**   **effect**
>
> *Mika drinks coffee @ 10 p.m.* ⟶ *she is awake most of the night*

2 🎧 2.6 Listen to the second part of the lecture. Match the causes in the left column with the effects in the right column.

1 Multiphasic sleep means people take many naps so

2 Multiphasic sleep makes you tired all the time and

3 Multiphasic sleep for weeks or months means that

a people can get sick.

b they never sleep for a long time.

c as a result people can have accidents.

E Critical thinking

Discuss the questions.

1 Which sleep pattern do you have? Is it always the same, or does it change?

2 Which sleep pattern do you think is best for these jobs:

airplane pilot   athlete   teacher   writer

3 Why do you think a multiphasic sleep cycle can make people sick?

Pronunciation for listening

Intonation in statements

Intonation means the way a speaker's voice moves up and down. Statements in English have *falling intonation*. At the end of a sentence, the speaker's voice goes up on the last stressed syllable of the sentence. Then the voice goes down lower than before. This fall tells listeners that the statement or idea is finished.

The last stressed syllable can be in the last word in the sentence or in an earlier word.

*Today we're going to continue talking about circadian **rhy**thm.*

*The time difference between New York and Beijing is **12** hours.*

1 🎧 **2.7** Listen to the following pairs of statements. Choose the statement which has the correct intonation.

   1 a I'm feeling a little tired.
      b I'm feeling a little tired.
   2 a Daniel usually studies at night.
      b Daniel usually studies at night.
   3 a Dinner is at 6 o'clock.
      b Dinner is at 6 o'clock.
   4 a I have an appointment.
      b I have an appointment.
   5 a It's really cold today.
      b It's really cold today.
   6 a Please work with a partner.
      b Please work with a partner.

2 Predict the final intonation in these sentences. Draw rising and falling arrows.

   1 Dina never eats breakfast.
   2 After lunch I often feel sleepy.
   3 Sam always uses an alarm clock.
   4 If the weather is nice, I take the bus to school.

Vocabulary development

Words for waking and sleeping

1 Match the words in the box with the correct definition.

early	fall asleep	get up	go to bed	late	stay up	tired	wake up

1 _____ (adj) near the beginning of a time period, or before the usual time

2 _____ (adj) the feeling that you need to rest and want to sleep

3 _____ (v) to finish your day and enter your bed

4 _____ (v) to get out of bed

5 _____ (v) to go from being awake to being asleep

6 _____ (v) to go to bed later than usual

7 _____ (v) to open your eyes in the morning

8 _____ (adj) after the correct or usual time

2 Complete the questions with the words and phrases from Exercise 1. Some sentences have more than one correct answer.

1 What time do you normally finish your activities and _____ at night?

2 What time do you normally _____ in the morning?

3 If you are _____ in the afternoon, do you take a nap?

4 Do you usually _____ as soon as you wake up in the morning?

5 Are you often early or _____ for lectures or meetings with friends?

6 Do you prefer to eat dinner _____, around 6, or late, around 9 or 10?

7 Do you usually _____ as soon as you close your eyes at night? If not, how long does it take you?

8 Is it easy or difficult for you to _____ late if you need to study?

3 Work with a partner. Ask and answer the questions in Exercise 2.

Academic words

1 Match the words in bold with the correct definition.

1	**biology** (n)	a	people who work for no money
2	**culture** (n)	b	the study of living things
3	**experts** (n)	c	a piece of paper that gives information about something it is fixed to
4	**energy** (n)		
5	**volunteers** (n)	d	the ideas and beliefs of a group of people
6	**label** (n)	e	the thing that makes people active
		f	people who know a lot about a subject

2 Complete the sentences with the words in bold from Exercise 1.

1 In American _____, it is common for people to eat dinner at 10 p.m.

2 In 2015, _____ was the third most popular university subject in the U.K.

3 In 2016, only about 10% of U.S. teenagers spent time as _____, for example, helping in hospitals, cleaning parks, or teaching young children.

4 One study showed that working people have the most _____ on Mondays and Tuesdays.

5 According to _____, dolphins and whales sleep with only half their brain at a time.

6 Read the washing instructions on the _____.

3 Work with a partner. Read the sentences in Exercise 2. Decide if they are true or false.

Speaking model

You are going to learn about adverbs of frequency, getting attention and asking for permission, and pronouncing word stress and intonation in questions. You are then going to use these to conduct a survey about people's sleeping and waking routine.

A Analyze

Complete the conversation with the phrases in the box.

1 When do you usually wake up in the morning?	4 How do you feel if you stay up late?
	5 When do you usually go to bed?
2 How do you usually feel in the morning?	6 Are you a day person or a night person?
3 Can I ask you some questions?	7 How often do you take naps?

A: Excuse me. I'm doing a survey for my class. _____?

B: Sure, no problem.

A: _____?

B: I usually wake up around 6:30 or 7 a.m. I have early classes almost every day.

A: And _____?

B: Around 11 p.m.

A: OK. Next question. _____?

B: I never take naps. It's impossible for me to fall asleep during the daytime.

A: All right. _____?

B: I always feel good in the morning. I have a lot of energy then.

A: _____?

B: Not good.

A: Finally, _____?

B: I am definitely a day person.

A: Well, thanks for your time.

B: You're welcome.

B Discuss

Work with a partner. Answer the questions.

1 How does Speaker A ask for permission? What else could they say?

2 Which question does Speaker A ask first about Speaker B's routine? Which one is last? Is it possible to change the order of the questions?

3 How does Speaker A end the conversation? How does Speaker B respond?

Grammar

Adverbs of frequency

Adverbs of frequency tell us how often something happens.

100%	50%	0%

always   usually   often   sometimes   rarely   never

    almost always   almost never

- Frequency adverbs come after *be* and before other verbs in simple present statements.
- *Sometimes* and *usually* can also come at the beginning of a sentence.
- Frequency adverbs come after the subject in simple present questions.

Affirmative: *Sandra always wakes up early. Carlos is rarely late to class.*

Negative: *Joseph doesn't always eat breakfast. We don't usually stay up late.*

Question: *Are you often hungry at night? When does she usually eat dinner?*

1 Complete the sentences and questions with the frequency adverb in parentheses. Some sentences have more than one correct answer.

(always) Aynur wakes up early. Aynur always wakes up early.

1 (never) Attila uses an alarm clock to wake up.
2 (sometimes) I forget to eat breakfast.
3 (rarely) Katya is in class before 10 a.m.
4 (often) Do you stay up late to study?
5 (usually) When do you study in the library?
6 (almost never) My roommate and I eat lunch together.
7 (almost always) Dan falls asleep quickly.

2 Look at the weekly schedule for a student named Ali. Use frequency adverbs to describe his routine. Some sentences have more than one correct answer.

	Su	M	T	W	Th	F	Sa
1 go to bed early							
2 wake up early		X	X	X	X	X	X
3 eat breakfast	X						
4 take a nap		X			X		
5 walk to school		X		X	X	X	
6 study with a friend	X		X		X		

3 Write five sentences about your daily routine. Use frequency adverbs.

Speaking skill

English has informal and formal ways of asking for permission. Use informal expressions for talking with friends, family, or classmates. Use formal expressions for talking with people you do not know well or with people in a high position. You may need to get your listener's attention before you ask for permission.

Getting attention	Asking for permission	
Excuse me.	*Is it OK if I sit here?*	*informal*
May I interrupt?	*Can I ask you a question?*	↓
	Could I use your book?	*formal*

1 **2.8 Listen and complete the sentences. Work with a partner. Discuss if they are formal or informal.**

1 It's raining. _____ use your umbrella?
   Sure, no problem.

2 _____ interrupt, Professor. _____ talk to you for a minute?
   I'm sorry, I have a meeting now. But I can talk to you later.

3 _____. _____ if I sit here?
   I'm sorry. I'm saving the seat for my friend.

4 _____ use your tablet?
   Sure, go ahead.

5 _____ borrow your dictionary?
   Yes, of course.

2 **Role play with a partner. Get attention and ask for permission in these situations.**

1 You are doing a survey. You want to ask your classmate a question.

2 It's cold in your office. Ask the other workers if it's OK to close the window.

3 Your teacher is working in his office. You have a question. Ask for permission to enter.

4 You have a doctor's appointment. Ask your professor if you can leave class early.

5 You are in a crowded cafeteria. Ask some students if you can sit at their table.

6 You want to use your friend's phone because you left yours at home.

A: Pardon me. Is it OK if I sit here?   *B: Of course. Have a seat.*

Pronunciation for speaking

Stress and intonation in questions

Yes/no questions have rising intonation. This means the voice rises on the last stressed syllable and then keeps on rising until the end of the sentence.

*Do you have a problem with **jet** lag?*

Sometimes the last stressed syllable is the last word in the sentence.

*Do you need to take a **nap**?*

Wh- questions have a rising–falling intonation. The voice goes up on the last stressed syllable and then goes down.

*Why do some people experience **jet** lag?*

1 🎧 **2.9** Listen to the questions. Draw arrows to show rising and falling intonation. Then listen again and repeat the sentences.

   1 Can I ask you some questions?
   2 What time do you go to bed?
   3 What time do you wake up?
   4 Do you feel tired?
   5 How much sleep do you need?

2 Rearrange the words to form questions. Underline the last stressed syllable. Draw arrows to show rising and falling intonation.

   1 you – need – alarm clock – do – an
      Do you need an alarm clock?

   2 what – to study – your – is – best – time of day
      _____

   3 jet lag – problem – is – for you – a
      _____

   4 how often – you – take – do – naps
      _____

   5 are – morning person – a – you
      _____

3 Ask and answer the questions in Exercise 2 with a partner.

Speaking task

You work for an organization that conducts surveys. You will conduct a survey about people's sleeping and waking routine.

Brainstorm

Write four extra topics you could ask about. Use the information from the unit and your own ideas.

wake up	eat breakfast	take a nap	go to sleep
_____	_____	_____	_____

Plan

Look back at your brainstorm and write six survey questions. Be sure to include:

- expressions for getting attention and asking permission
- questions in simple present
- adverbs of frequency
- vocabulary from pages 36, 38, and 39

1 _____

2 _____

3 _____

4 _____

5 _____

6 _____

Speak

Conduct your survey. Take notes on your partner's answers.

Share

Sit in groups. Tell your classmates about the person you surveyed. Tell the group if the person is a "day person" or a "night person."

I surveyed (person's name). She wakes up … She doesn't eat … She often feels …
She never … I think she is a day/night person.

Reflect

Discuss the questions with a partner:

- When is the best time to go to sleep?
- When is the best time to study?

Review

Wordlist

MACMILLAN
DICTIONARY

Vocabulary preview

active (adj)***	expect (v)***	period (n)***
awake (adj)*	find out (v)	regular (adj)***
brain (n)***	healthy (adj)***	total (n)***
choices (n)***	interrupt (v)**	typical (adj)***
cycle (n)**	natural (adj)***	
daily (adj)***	pattern (n)***	

Vocabulary development

early (adj)***	go to bed (phrase)	tired (adj)***
fall asleep (phrase)	late (adj)***	wake up (phrasal v)
get up (phrasal v)	stay up (phrasal v)	

Academic words

biology (n)*	energy (n)***	label (n)***
culture (n)***	expert (n)***	volunteer (n)**

Academic words review

Complete the sentences with the words in the box.

believe	energy	expert	volunteer	positive

1 Many people _____ that watching TV helps you fall asleep.
2 Professor Malik is an _____ on sleep patterns. She knows everything.
3 I am a _____ at my local school. I teach English and Biology.
4 I'm a pretty _____ person, I'm not one of those negative types.
5 I have lots of_____ in the morning and not so much at night.

Unit review

Listening 1		I can listen for specific information.
Listening 2		I can listen for effects.
Vocabulary		I can use words to describe waking and sleeping.
Grammar		I can use adverbs of frequency.
Speaking		I can get a person's attention and ask for permission.
Pronunciation		I can pronounce stress and intonation in questions.

Discussion point

Mark the sentences
T (True) or *F* (False).

1 Price is the most important feature of university accommodation. ___

2 Less than half of students prefer to live off campus. ___

3 Over 80% of students are happy to share a kitchen. ___

Discuss the question.

Is it better to live on campus or off campus? Why?

Student survey
The best university accommodation

Top three most important features of university accommodation

1 Fast internet connection   **2** Price   **3** Close to university

 Location

55% of students prefer to live off campus

32% of students want to live near a shopping mall

When do students find accommodation?

 Most students find accommodation between **August** and **September**

Rooms

75% of students prefer to have their own bedroom

82% of students are happy to share a kitchen

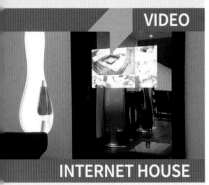

VIDEO

INTERNET HOUSE

Before you watch

Discuss the questions with a partner.

1 How many apps do you have on your smartphone and what do they do?
   I have about … apps on my phone.   I have one app which …

2 What objects are controlled by a smartphone or computer in your home?
   My … is controlled by an app on my phone.

3 What other type of things could you control in your home from a remote control or smartphone?
   I think you could control …

UNIT
AIMS

LISTENING 1 Identifying speaker attitude
LISTENING 2 Predicting
STUDY SKILL Listening skills

VOCABULARY Adjectives to describe places
GRAMMAR Comparative and superlative adjectives
SPEAKING Giving your opinion

A university library.

While you watch

Watch the video. Put these objects in the order that you see them.

___ electronic fire

___ coffee maker

___ TV screen moving up slowly

___ someone using an app on a tablet

___ remote controls

_1_ coffee table with built-in computer screen

After you watch

Work with a partner. Discuss the questions.

1   What was your favorite piece of technology from the video? Why?

    My favorite piece of technology was the …

2   Is technology in the home a good idea? Why? / Why not?

    I think technology in the home is a good/bad idea because …

Campus housing

A Vocabulary preview

1   Match the words in bold with the correct definition.

1	**accommodation** (n)	a	unhappy because you are alone
2	**convenient** (adj)	b	a place for someone to stay, live, or work in
3	**independent** (adj)	c	easy and does not cause problems
4	**lonely** (adj)	d	prefer to do things yourself
5	**advantage** (n)	e	something that you can choose
6	**brochure** (n)	f	places or equipment for people to use
7	**facilities** (n)	g	something that makes one thing better than something else
8	**options** (n)	h	a small book with pictures and information

2   Complete the sentences below with the words in bold from Exercise 1.

1   I am a very _____ person. I prefer to work on my own.

2   The place where I live is _____ for getting to school.

3   I have a lot of hobbies and friends, so I don't ever feel _____.

4   Most students in my country live in _____ that is off campus.

5   Before I book a holiday, I carefully read the _____ about it.

6   I don't like to have too many _____ because I'm not very good at making decisions.

7   My school has a lot of _____ that students can use, like a gym.

8   Learning about a new culture is the biggest _____ of speaking a foreign language.

3   Work with a partner. Which of the sentences are true for you?

B Before you listen

Activating prior knowledge

1   Look at the pictures of three types of university accommodation rooms. Which one do you prefer? Discuss with a partner.

My favorite room is … because …

2   What are some advantages of on-campus and off-campus student accommodation?

Advantages: on campus	Advantages: off campus
Close to university buildings	*More independent*

C Global listening

🎧 **3.1** Listen to part of a conversation. Benito, Miki, and Dennis are discussing their options for university accommodation. Draw lines to match each student with the name, location, and type of accommodation.

Student	Accommodation	Location	Type
1 Dennis	Ivy Suites	near the gym	traditional dorm
2 Miki	Hillside Terrace	near the library	homestay
3 Benito	Nelson Hall	near the mall	apartment

Traditional dorm

Apartment

Homestay

D Close listening

People can express their attitude, preference, or opinion about places, things, people, and ideas with various phrases:

I prefer …	*I agree (with you)*
I (don't) like / want …	*I think so, too*
I'd rather …	*I feel the same way*
I'm (not) interested in / I'm (not) keen on …	*I don't agree / I disagree*

1 🎧 **3.2** Listen to the conversation. Complete each sentence with one word.

1 Benito: It's really hard to decide which type of accommodation to live in.
   Miki: I _____, Benito.

2 Miki: Really, why?
   Dennis: Well, I _____ to live on campus because it's safer…

3 Dennis: I also think the area around the library is quieter and more attractive.
   Miki: Yes, I _____ so, too.

4 Benito: The cafeteria has the worst food on campus.
   Dennis: I _____.

5 Benito: Miki, which accommodation are you interested in?
   Miki: I _____ Ivy Suites.

2 🎧 **3.3** Listen to more of the conversation. Choose the correct option.

1 Ivy Suites has a convenience store on **each floor / the first floor.**

2 Ivy Suites costs **$920/ $850** a month.

3 Hillside Terrace is more convenient for **shopping / studying**.

4 At Hillside Terrace, the student gets a **shared / private** room.

5 Hillside Terrace costs **$815 / $850** a month.

E Critical thinking

Discuss the questions.

1 What do you like about your house or apartment?

2 Do college students in your country prefer to live in university accommodation on campus, private accommodation off campus, or at home? Why?

3 Put the following items in order of importance when choosing university accommodation. Discuss your answers with a partner.

   Price   Location   Facilities   Size   Safety   Transportation

Study skills | Reflection: Listening skills

In your journal, consider how well you listen to others. Do you:
- listen carefully to what other people say?
- give other people time to speak?
- let other people finish before you start?
- use encouraging non-verbal signals, such as eye-contact?

Could you do anything differently to make others more comfortable when they are speaking?

© Stella Cottrell (2013)

1 Describe your home to your partner. Include the following information:
- the size (number of rooms)
- the location (what is it near)
- the type (is it a house, an apartment, etc.)

2 Work with your partner. Read the list below. Check the skills you followed.

___ I listened carefully to what my partner said.

___ I gave my partner time to speak.

___ I let my partner finish before speaking.

___ I looked at my partner when he/she was speaking.

3 Tell your partner what you remember about their home.

Less is more

A Vocabulary preview

1 Match the words in bold with the correct definition.

1	**visitor** (n)	a	relating to a town or city
2	**mobile home** (n)	b	an empty or available area
3	**urban** (adj)	c	a person who comes to see you, often a friend or family member
4	**space** (n)		
5	**tiny** (adj)	d	a place where you live that isn't fixed to one location
6	**fold up** (v)	e	a particular style or design of an item, such as a car or home
7	**model** (n)		
8	**ready-made** (adj)	f	already complete so you can use it immediately
		g	to reduce the size of something
		h	very small

2 Complete the sentences below with the words and phrases in bold from Exercise 1.

1 A student like me doesn't need much _____ for a room, 10 square meters is enough.

2 My room is so small, it's really_____.

3 I would rather live in an _____ area because there are many things to do in a city.

4 The _____ of home I prefer is traditional with a large garden.

5 In my country, it's normal for a _____ to bring a gift when they come to your home.

6 My bed can _____ in my room, which is great because it makes more space.

7 I don't know how to cook, so I often eat _____ meals.

8 I would like to live in a _____ so I can take my home with me if I move cities.

3 Work with a partner. Which of the sentences in Exercise 2 are true for you?

B Before you listen

Activating prior knowledge

1 What is the smallest room you could live in?

The smallest room I could live in is …

2 What eight items do you think are essential to live in a very small home?

For me, the items I would need are …

C Global listening

Before you listen to a news report, lecture, or presentation, you can use information like the title and pictures, to help you predict or guess the main ideas. You can also predict some of the key words that you will hear so that you can better understand the listening text.

Predicting

1 Look at the title on page 50 and pictures below. Answer the questions.

1 What do you predict the main idea will be?

Main idea: _____

2 Do you think the report will give a positive or negative opinion of tiny homes? Why?

Opinion: _____

3 What key words will you hear in *Less is more*?

Key words: _____

2 🎧 3.4 Listen to *Less is more* and check your predictions.

3 🎧 3.4 Listen again and number the topics in the order they are discussed.

A ___ Different models of mini houses

B ___ Advantages of very small homes

C ___ Cost of Carlos and Marta's home

D _1_ Why tiny homes are popular

E ___ Items inside Carlos and Marta's home

D Close listening

1 🎧 **3.5** Listen to Carlos' description of the tiny house. Put the items in the box into the correct column.

| bath | bed | books | CDs | cupboard | shower | tablet | TV |

Items they have	Items they don't have

Predicting

2 Read the notes below. With a partner, predict if the answer will be a word or number for each blank.

- Bought home ready-made from Mini House Solutions
- MHS: sells homes 5– ^{1}_____ sq ms.
- Choice of ^{2}_____ different models.
- Can deliver with wheels
- Owners can park: urban areas, field, forest, river, on the ^{3}_____ of a truck
- Carlos and Marta's home = $ ^{4}_____
- Marta: mini-home uses fewer materials / less energy; ^{5}_____ to environment

3 🎧 **3.6** Listen to the second part of *Less is more*. Complete the summary with one word or a number on each line.

E Critical thinking

Discuss the questions.

1 Would you like to live in a tiny home? Why/Why not?

I would/wouldn't like to live in a tiny home because …

2 What are the benefits of living in a tiny home? What are the disadvantages?

The benefits of living in a tiny home are …

The disadvantages of living in a tiny home are …

3 Do you think a tiny home is a good type of university accommodation? Why/Why not?

I think a tiny home is a good/bad idea because …

Pronunciation for listening

/s/ and /z/

The written letter **s** is sometimes pronounced as /s/ and sometimes as /z/. The following words are pronounced with an /s/ sound:

class, house, interested, possible, safe

The following words are pronounced with a /z/ sound:

design, has, please, visitor, words

In English, the sound /z/ is voiced. This means we use our vocal cords when we say a word which contains this sound. The sound /s/ is unvoiced. This means we don't use our vocal cords when we say a word which contains this sound.

Touch your throat and pronounce the words in the list above that have the /z/ sound. You should feel a small vibration. Do the same thing with the words in the list above that have the /s/ sound. You shouldn't feel a small vibration.

1 🎧 **3.7** Listen to the following sentences and complete each blank with one word.

    1 They're _____ to downsize their idea of home.

    2 And _____ a cupboard above and another below the bed.

    3 _____ Lee is an expert in this area.

    4 She _____ that many people believe a simple life is important for _____.

    5 Not only that, it's _____ cozy – very cozy!

2 Read the sentences above with a partner. How does your partner pronounce the letter "s" in each sentence? Mark the letter "s" with either /s/ or /z/ in each sentence.

3 🎧 **3.7** Listen to the sentences again. Does the letter "s" have an /s/ or /z/ sound? Mark the letter "s" with either /s/ or /z/ in each sentence.

Vocabulary development

Adjectives to describe places

1 Match the adjectives on the left with their opposites on the right.

1	safe	a	near
2	far	b	traditional
3	modern	c	boring
4	interesting	d	dangerous
5	cheap	e	noisy
6	quiet	f	unknown
7	large	g	small
8	popular	h	expensive

2 Choose the correct adjective to complete the review of Forrest Flowers.

🏠 Review: My accommodation

Hi everyone! My name's Michael and I live in Forrest Flowers. I want to give some advice to new students thinking about moving in here. Well first, it's **cheap/expensive**! Only $725 per month, which is less than all the other accommodation. Forrest Flowers is quite **modern/traditional**, I believe it was built in 2006, and the rooms are very nicely presented and they are **small/large** so you have lots of space for your stuff. It's also in a really nice area without any traffic so it's super **quiet/noisy**. You have lots of things to do around here, including cafés, restaurants and a cinema, so it's never **interesting/boring**. There is one disadvantage, however, and that's the distance to campus. It's **near/far** from the university. It takes 15 minutes by car or one hour by bike, if you're feeling adventurous!

3 Read the review of Forrest Flowers again. Would you like to live there?

4 Describe where you live to your partner. Use the adjectives in Exercise 1. Think about:

distance to school/university	size	transportation	facilities	safety

I live in … I really like it because it's … One disadvantage is …

Academic words

1 Read the sentences. Match the words in bold with the correct definitions below.

1 All the building materials are sold with plans and simple **instructions**.

2 Marta and Carlos attempt to live comfortably on the smallest **site** possible.

3 Our home uses fewer materials and less energy, and so it's friendlier to the **environment**.

4 The price of Forrest Flowers is **similar** to Nelson Hall.

5 MHS **design** mini-homes from 5 to 35 square meters.

6 There are three different models **available**.

a _____ (n) something possible to get, use, or buy

b _____ (v) to decide and draw or describe how something is made, including what it looks like

c _____ (n) air, water, buildings, and animals that are around us

d _____ (n) an area of land where something is built

e _____ (adj) having many things in common, but not exactly the same

f _____ (n) information explaining how to do or make something

2 Complete each sentence with a word in bold from Exercise 1.

1 Would you like to _____ your own home? Why / Why not?

2 What kinds of university accommodation are _____ to students in your country?

3 Are you good at following _____ from your teacher, boss, or sports coach?

4 Is there a noisy construction _____ near your school or office?

5 Do you live in a _____ type of accommodation to your friends?

6 What projects are there to help the _____ in your country?

3 Answer the questions above and explain your answers to a partner.

Actually, I would like to design a cinema room for my home with …

Speaking model

You are going to compare three types of university accommodation and choose the best one.

A Analyze

Read the model text and complete the table with the correct information.

	Kent Hall	Hillcrest	Bridge House
Location	1 km from uni	[1]_____ km from uni	[2]_____ km from uni
Size	8 floors / 38 rooms	6 floors / 28 rooms	5 floors / 22 rooms
Room size	18 m²	25 m²	[3]_____ m²
Internet	[4]_____ Mb/s	17.5 Mb/s	20.6 Mb/s
Safety	7 crimes per yr	4 crimes per yr	1 crime per yr
Cost	$750 month	[5] $_____ month	$1150 month

Mia: Which student accommodation do you like best?

Pablo: I like the design of Bridge House. It has larger rooms than Hillcrest and Kent Hall.

Mia: That's true. 38 square meters is very big. But in my opinion Hillcrest is more attractive.

Pablo: I disagree. I prefer Bridge House's more traditional design.

Rosa: I think that Kent Hall is the most attractive, and with 24.3Mb/s, it has the fastest internet speed.

Pablo: I'd rather live in safer accommodation. Bridge House has the least crime.

Rosa: True. However its location is the least convenient.

Mia: You're right. 3 km is far away. Bridge House is also the most expensive.

Pablo: That's a good point, but I think it's in the most interesting area.

Rosa: I don't agree. I think Hillcrest has the best facilities and it's only 0.5 km from the university.

Mia: And the price is $840 per month.

B Discuss

Discuss the questions with a partner.

1 Which accommodation in the dialogue do you think is best? Why?

2 Describe the best kind of student accommodation in your country.

Grammar

Comparatives and superlative adjectives

Structure	Form	Example
Comparatives One-syllable adjectives Adjectives ending in -y Adjectives with two or more syllables	Adjective + -er + than y ⟶ -ier + than more/less + adjective	It's safer than the area around the gym. Perhaps cozier than may people want. It's more modern than Nelson Hall.
Superlatives One syllable adjectives Adjectives ending in -y Adjectives with two or more syllables	The + adjective + -est -y ⟶ -iest The most/the least + adjective	It's the cheapest accommodation I think that it has the tastiest food on campus. It's the most expensive place to live.
Exceptions Some adjectives don't follow the rules above	good ⟶ better ⟶ the best bad ⟶ worse ⟶ the worst ar ⟶ further ⟶ the furthest	Ivy Suites is the best accommodation. Hillcrest is worse than Nelson Hall. Bridge House is the furthest from university.

1 Complete the table with correct forms of the adjectives.

Adjective	Comparative	Superlative
small	1_____	the smallest
safe	2_____	the safest
quiet	quieter	3_____
modern	more modern	4_____
noisy	noisier	5_____
traditional	6_____	the most traditional
convenient	more convenient	7_____

2 Complete each sentence with the correct form of the adjective.

1 Kent Hall is (tall) _____ than Hillcrest.

2 Kent Hall has the (large) _____ rooms.

3 The internet in Bridge House is (fast) _____ than the internet in Kent Hall.

4 The internet in Hillcrest is the (slow) _____.

5 Kent Hall is (safe) _____ than Bridge House.

6 Kent Hall is the (cheap) _____ dorm.

7 Hillcrest is the (expensive) _____ accommodation.

8 Hillcrest is (close) _____ to the university than Bridge House.

Speaking skill

You can give your opinion with the following expressions:

I think/believe (that) …   *In my opinion …*   *It's my opinion that …*

You can agree or disagree with someone's opinion with the following expressions:

Agree	Disagree
I agree (with you).	*I disagree (with you).*
You're right.	*I don't agree.*
I think so too.	*I don't think so.*

1 Write the phrases in the box below under the correct headings.

> Yes, that's true.   I have a different opinion.   For me …
> I'm not sure about that.   In my view …   I feel the same way.
> That's a good point.   I don't quite agree.   I'd say that …

Give an opinion	Agree	Disagree
_____	_____	_____
_____	_____	_____
_____	_____	_____

2 Read the opinions in the table below. Do you agree or disagree with each statement? Check the box that matches your opinion.

Opinion	Strongly agree	Agree	Disagree	Strongly disagree
1 The best accommodation is usually on campus.				
2 It's more interesting for students to live off campus.				
3 A food market must be five minutes from the accommodation.				
4 A 20 minute walk to school is no problem for me.				
5 Student accommodation usually has terrible food.				

3 Work with a partner. Take turns giving your opinion about the statements in the table above. Agree or disagree with your partner.

Pronunciation for speaking

Linking consonants to vowels

When a word ends in a consonant and the following word starts with a vowel, the consonant sound is linked with the vowel sound.

there's another... *interested in...* *not keen on...*

1 🔊 **3.8** Underline final consonant sounds followed by initial vowels. Then listen and notice the pronunciation.

1 I'm quite interested in Nelson Hall.
2 I'm not keen on living far from the university.
3 How much is the rent?
4 How much does it cost?
5 What does Carlos think about their living space?
6 I keep books on my tablet.
7 There's enough space for cupboards.
8 In other words, they're choosing to downsize.

2 Read the sentences with a partner. Focus on linking final consonants to initial vowels.

3 Work in groups of three. Read the model text. Focus on linking final consonants to initial vowels.

Mia: Which student accommodation do you like best?

Pablo: I like the design of Bridge House. It has larger rooms than Hillcrest and Kent Hall.

Mia: That's true. 38 square meters is very big. But in my opinion Hillcrest is more attractive.

Pablo: I disagree. I prefer Bridge House's more traditional design.

Rosa: I think that Kent Hall is the most attractive, and with 24.3Mb/s, it has the fastest internet speed.

Pablo: I'd rather live in safer accommodation. Bridge House has the least crime.

Rosa: True. However its location is the least convenient.

Mia: You're right. 3 km is far away. Bridge House is also the most expensive.

Pablo: That's a good point but I think it's in the most interesting area.

Rosa: I don't agree. I think Hillcrest has the best facilities and it's only 0.5 km from the university.

Mia: And the price is $840 per month.

Speaking task

Compare three types of university accommodation.

Brainstorm

Make a list of five important features for you when choosing university accommodation.

1 _____ 3 _____ 5 _____

2 _____ 4 _____

Choose your university accommodation

	Mayfair Hall	Century Tower	Sunny Cottage
Location	on campus: 0.7 km from Uni bldg	1.5 km from campus: next to shopping mall	3 km from campus: near bus stop; Green Park
Size	6 floors / 40 rooms	4 floors / 24 apartments	1 floor / 1 room
Rooms	double: 2 st. per room 30 sq. m	3 ppl. per apt; 1 st. per room 35 sq. m	single or double 48 sq. m (whole house)
Facilities	cafeteria; laundry room Library w/free coffee two shower rooms on each floor	share kitchen & bathroom TV room w/gaming gym on 4th fl. 24h security	mini-kitchen & shower free shuttle bus view of lake and park
Internet	27.3 Mb/s	24.1 Mb/s	40 Mb/s
Cost	$850 month	$775 month	$1,200 month

Plan

Work with a partner. Compare the three types of university accommodation. Use the comparative form and the superlative form (page 57).

Speak

Choose the best accommodation and tell your partner. Use phrases for giving an opinion (page 58) and give reasons.

Share

Form a group. Compare your ideas. Do you agree with your group?

Reflect

What makes the best university accommodation?

Review

Wordlist

MACMILLAN
DICTIONARY

Vocabulary preview

accommodation (n)**	independent (adj)***	space (n)***
advantage (n)***	lonely (adj)**	tiny (adj)***
brochure (n)*	mobile home (n)	urban (adj)
convenient (adj)**	model (n)***	visitor (n)***
facilities (n)***	options (n)***	
fold up (phrasal v)	ready-made (adj)	

Vocabulary development

boring (adj)**	large (adj)***	safe (adj)***
cheap (adj)***	modern (adj)***	small (adj)***
dangerous (adj)***	near (adj/adv)***	traditional (adj)***
expensive (adj)***	noisy (adj)*	unknown (adj)**
far (adj/adv)***	popular (adj)***	
interesting (adj)***	quiet (adj)***	

Academic words

available (adj)***	environment (n)***	site (n)***
design (n)***	instructions (n)***	similar (adj)***

Academic words review

Complete the sentences with the words in the box.

available	culture	environment	grades	volunteer

1 The house uses all the _____ space. Everything is there for a reason.
2 In my _____, we always take gifts when we visit someone's home.
3 Using less energy is good for the _____.
4 Some students _____ to help out around campus.
5 My _____ improved after I went to the library to study.

Unit review

Listening 1	I can identify the speaker's attitude.
Listening 2	I can predict information.
Vocabulary	I can use adjectives to describe places.
Grammar	I can use comparative and superlative adjectives.
Speaking	I can give my opinion.
Pronunciation	I can link consonants to vowels.

Smarter Cities

Discussion point

Study the infographic and the sentences. Write *T* (True) or *F* (False).

1 Smart street lights can turn on or off according to the number of people on the street.

2 Free wi-fi is only available at train stations.

3 People can get traffic updates on their smartphones.

Discuss the question.

Which of these features does your town or city have?

1 **Green buildings:** gardens on the roofs of buildings

2 **Traffic information:** instant traffic updates to people's smartphones to help them plan

3 **Earthquake detection:** tells people where an earthquake might happen

4 **Wi-fi:** free wi-fi in all public places

5 **Smart roads:** fast and slow lanes that can change according to the number of cars, people walking, and bicycles

6 **Smart street lights:** can turn on or off according to the weather

7 **Mixed-use buildings:** with shops on the street level and apartments above

8 **Fast, cheap public transportation:** including subways, light rail, buses and ferries

---

VIDEO

ROOF GARDEN

Before you watch

Match the words in bold with the correct definition.

1 **roof** (n)   a a large shop divided into smaller shops
2 **department store** (n)   b a planned piece of work
3 **view** (n)   c the highest part of something
4 **project** (n)   d the top of a building, often on the outside
5 **top** (n)   e things you can see from a window

UNIT AIMS

LISTENING 1 Listening for corrections
LISTENING 2 Listening for advantages and disadvantages
STUDY SKILL Using information from lectures

VOCABULARY Words to describe cities
GRAMMAR Present progressive for changes over time
SPEAKING Giving reasons for or against something

Downtown Los Angeles.

While you watch

Watch the video. Choose the correct number to complete each sentence.

1 The size of the rooftop is **600 / 700** square meters.

2 There are **20 / 200** employees of the department store who are interested in gardening.

3 Charlotte Arnoux has about **10 / 20** eggplants in her garden.

4 The Paris city government wants to have lots of rooftop gardens, by the year **2020 / 2025**.

5 In the future, Paris will have **100 / 1000** hectares of green roofs, sidewalks and walls.

After you watch

Work with a partner. Discuss the questions.

1 Do you like the idea of rooftop gardens?
Yes, I like this idea because …
No, I don't like the idea because …

2 Does your city have rooftop gardens?
Yes, my city has a rooftop garden in …

3 In what other public places is it a good idea to have gardens and plants?
I think it's a good to have them in … / near … / on … / at … because …

Los Angeles: A changing city

A Vocabulary preview

1 Match the words in bold with the correct definition.

1	**trend** (n)	a	not private; owned or used by all people
2	**public** (adj)	b	connected things that work together
3	**system** (n)	c	having different parts, purposes, people etc.
4	**mixed** (adj)	d	a change that becomes popular
5	**level** (n)	e	very big
6	**crowded** (adj)	f	to become larger, taller, longer, etc.
7	**grow** (v)	g	too many people
8	**huge** (adj)	h	a floor of a building

2 Complete the sentences with the words in bold from Exercise 1.

1 My neighborhood has many different kinds of people: families, single people, old and young people. I really enjoy living in a _____ neighborhood.

2 Seoul, Korea, has an excellent transportation _____. It is clean, safe, and fast.

3 Guadalajara, Mexico, has one of the largest _____ parks in the world. It has more than 3 million visitors each year.

4 An interesting _____ in many American cities is that apartments are getting smaller and smaller.

5 My school building has three floors. You enter from the street _____. You go downstairs to the cafeteria and upstairs to the classrooms.

6 Shanghai and Beijing are _____ cities, but my city, Zibo, is much smaller.

7 My family love plants. They _____ about ten different kinds of flowers.

8 I live in a big city so the city center is often _____ with tourists at weekends.

3 Work with a partner. Answer the questions.

1 Does your town or city have a good transportation system?

2 What is the tallest building in your city? How many floors does it have?

3 Apartments are getting smaller and smaller in many cities in America. Is this trend the same in your country?

B Before you listen

Discuss the questions with a partner.

1 Los Angeles is in southern California, in the United States. It is on the Pacific Ocean. What might be some advantages of living in this place? Think about the weather and the geography.

Los Angeles is/has … One good thing is …

2 Los Angeles has more than 3 million people. The area around Los Angeles has more than 18 million people. What are some problems with living in a huge city?

One problem is … People have / don't have …

3 What else do you know about Los Angeles?

C Global listening

4.1 Listen to two university students talking about Los Angeles. Put the topics in the order that the students discuss them. The first one is done for you.

___ Urban gardens   ___ Where people lived in the past

_1_ Michelle's report   ___ Mixed-use buildings

___ The Los Angeles Metro system

Listening for corrections

D Close listening

> Sometimes a speaker makes a mistake when giving information. The listener might want to correct the mistake. For example:
>
> *Actually / In fact, I think …*   *Well, I read / heard that …*
> *No, that's not true. In fact …*   *No, that's wrong.*

1 **4.1** Listen and choose the best option to complete each sentence.

1 Public transportation is getting
   ¹ **worse and worse / better and better**.

2 Mixed-use buildings are ² **old / new** in Los Angeles.
3 In downtown Los Angeles, most of the people are
   ³ **homeless / families and professionals**.

4 Michelle, who wrote the report, thinks
   urban gardens are ⁴ **boring / fun**.

2 **4.1** Listen again and complete each sentence with one word or number.

1 The new Metro system has _____ lines.
2 You can take the Metro from downtown to the _____.
3 Mixed-use buildings have restaurants and shops on the street _____.
4 People in Los Angeles don't want to spend time in _____.
5 People are planting urban gardens in schools, parks, and on the roofs of _____.
6 Because California has nice weather, food can grow all _____.

E Critical thinking

Discuss the question.

Do you think urban gardens are a good idea in your city? Why / why not?
I think urban gardens are / aren't a good idea because …

Study skills | Using information from lectures

Lectures and other taught lessons are designed as useful starting points for your study. They give a general overview of the main ideas, theories, debates, and recent research in the subject.

<u>Before the lecture or class</u>

Look for themes, issues, and headings.

Write down questions you want answered.

Look through your notes from the previous class, and look for links with the next one.

<u>During the lecture or class</u>

Good teachers tell you at the beginning which main topics will be covered in which order. Use such information to help you structure your notes.

Note down headings, questions, points, and references provided during the session.

<u>After the lecture or class</u>

Label and file notes and handouts.

Read through your notes.

Discuss the lecture or class with others.

Compare notes.

© Stella Cottrell (2013)

1 Read about these students' problems when they go to class. How can they improve the way they use information from their lectures and classes?

1 It's terrible. I usually keep all my handouts in the back of my textbook and they always fall out everywhere. I should probably do something with them.

2 I don't want to write notes in my book because my brother is going to use this book next year after I've finished.

3 I never know what questions to ask in a lecture so I just keep quiet even when I don't understand what the teacher is saying.

4 I just borrow paper and a pen from the teacher. I can usually remember everything anyway.

5 I can never read afterwards what I wrote in class. I have to write so fast, my handwriting is really bad.

6 I don't know the other students in the class and I don't speak to them. I don't really need their help.

7 I just keep my book in a cupboard at the back of the class. I have too much to carry anyway—my computer, sunglasses, car keys, phone …

Wallscapes

A Vocabulary preview

Read the sentences. Match the words in bold with the correct definition.

1 When the weather is nice, we enjoy **outdoor** activities like hiking and bike-riding.

2 There are some **differences** between British and American English spelling.

3 At the Dubai Mall in the UAE, shoppers can buy every kind of **product**, like clothes, gold, and flowers.

4 The Eiffel Tower in Paris, France is over 300 meters tall. If you go to the **top**, you can see all of the city around you.

5 I am worried about water **pollution** in my country. The rivers and lakes are getting dirtier and dirtier.

a _____ (n) things that are not the same

b _____ (n) a thing that a company makes, and a thing that people buy and use

c _____ (adj) not in a house or building; in nature

d _____ (n) dirty air, water, land, etc.

e _____ (n) the highest place on a building, mountain, etc.

B Before you listen

Activating prior knowledge

1 Look at the three pictures. They show three types of outdoor advertising in cities. Write the letter of the image next to the type of advertising in the list below.

1 ___ billboard   2 ___ wallscape   3 ___ bus stop ad

A

Wi-fi System
Auto-breaking
Voice control

A car for all environments

2 Which advertisement do you like the best? Why?

I think the first/second/third ad is a...

I like the (billboard) ad the best because...

C Global listening

🎧 **4.2** Listen to *Wallscapes* and check (✓) the topics the speakers talk about.

✓ 1 A description of a wallscape

___ 2 Differences between a wallscape and a billboard

___ 3 Differences between a wallscape and a bus stop ad.

___ 4 Materials used to make wallscapes

___ 5 Workers who make wallscapes

___ 6 The advantages of wallscapes

___ 7 The disadvantages of wallscapes

___ 8 The history of wallscapes

Listening for main ideas

Listening for advantages
and disadvantages

D Close listening

An **advantage** or benefit is something that helps or makes it better.

One advantage (of wallscapes) is that they are huge, so they're easy to see.

A **disadvantage** is something that causes problems or difficulties.

A disadvantage is that a lot of people are against every kind of outdoor advertising.

Listen for words that help you identify advantages and disadvantages:

Advantages	Disadvantages
advantage	disadvantage
benefit	difficulty / problem
good point	bad point

🎧 **4.3** Listen and complete the notes below with one word or number.

1st advantage
    They are [1]_____. Can't miss them.
    One of biggest wallscapes = [2]_____ sq. ms, in Los Angeles
2nd advantage
    [3]_____ for people to remember products
1st disadvantage
    [4]_____. Companies have to pay to make it, put it up, and take it
        down.
    Also have to pay for space: $15,000 – $60,000 per [5]_____.
2nd disadvantage
    Some people against outdoor ad. Think it is a kind of [6]_____.

E Critical thinking

Discuss the questions.

1　In your city, what is a good location for a wallscape? Why?

2　Do you agree with Steve Engle that wallscapes are a kind of art?

3　Imagine that you are the president of a company that sells motorcycles. Is a wallscape a good way to advertise your products? Why or why not?

   A wallscape is / isn't a good way to advertise a motorcycle because …

Pronunciation for listening

Reduced forms 1

Notice the spelling of *Alaska*. It is written with three *a* vowels. The letters are the same, but they don't sound the same. We say aLAska, with stress on the second syllable. It is the only syllable with a full, clear "a" sound. The other two syllables are unstressed. They sound more like /ə/. We call this unstressed vowel sound *schwa*. The symbol for schwa is /ə/. Some short words are unstressed most of the time. That means the vowel is usually pronounced as schwa, and it can be hard to hear. For example:

Word	Stressed sound	Unstressed sound
and	/ænd/	/ən/
or	/ɔr/	/ər/
for	/fɔr/	/fər/
to	/tuw/	/tə/
are	/ɑr/	/ər/
of	/ʌv/	/ə/
a	/eɪ/	/ə/

1 🎧 **4.4** Listen to the excerpts below. Choose *S* (Stressed) if the underlined syllable is long and clear. Choose *U* (Unstressed) if it is unstressed and reduced.

1 It's my dream <u>to</u> go there.   S   U
2 Thanks <u>for</u> telling me about your report.   S   U
3 Six lines <u>are</u> already running.   S   U
4 Well, they <u>are</u> new in Los Angeles.   S   U
5 Public transportation is getting better <u>and</u> better.   S   U

2 Read the sentences. Underline the words from the skills box above with reduced vowels.

1 I decided to learn more about it.
2 It's a report for my urban studies class.
3 What other trends are happening in LA?
4 Mixed-use buildings have offices or apartments above.
5 I thought most of the people in downtown Los Angeles were homeless.
6 The city is working hard to solve that problem.
7 I have a lot of wrong ideas about Los Angeles.
8 Buildings are getting taller.

Vocabulary development

Words to describe cities

1 Match the definitions with the words in the box.

historic	neighborhood	parking	tourists

1 _____ (n) people who are visiting a place on vacation

2 _____ (n) a place where you can leave your car

3 _____ (n) a part of a town

4 _____ (adj) famous or important (building, event, etc.) from the past

business	downtown	popular	increase

5 _____ (adj) in the center of a city, close to offices and shopping

6 _____ (v) to go up

7 _____ (adj) liked or used by many people

8 _____ (n) a company or industry that sells services or products to make money

2 Complete the sentences with the words from the boxes in Exercise 1.

1 Do you like the _____ where you are living now? Why?

2 Is it hard to find _____ for your car in your city?

3 Someday, would you like to have your own _____ and be the boss?

4 In your city, what is the most _____ area where people like to visit?

5 Do you think the cost of public transportation will _____ next year?

6 How old is your hometown? Does it have _____ buildings?

7 What is the best time of year for _____ to visit your hometown?

8 Does your hometown have a _____ area? Is it expensive to live there? Why?

3 Work with a partner. Take turns asking and answering the questions in Exercise 2.

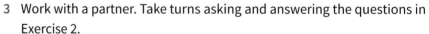

Academic words

1   Match the words in bold with the correct definition.

    1 **area** (n)   a   a piece of paper or file which contains information
    2 **channel** (n)   b   very big
    3 **enormous** (adj)   c   a part of a city or country
    4 **equipment** (n)   d   very clear to see or understand
    5 **document** (n)   e   a radio station or TV station
    6 **obvious** (adj)   f   tools and machines for a job or project

2   Complete each sentence with a word in bold from Exercise 1.

    1 In Mumbai, India, one family has a 27-story, 37,000-square-meter house. Would you like to own an _____ house like that?

    2 If a company wants to put up a wallscape, what kind of _____ does it need to use?

    3 What kind of _____ do you need to have to buy a house or car?

    4 Is it important for you to live near a green _____, such as a park or forest?

    5 What is a popular TV _____ in your country?

    6 Are the exit signs _____ in your school or office or are they difficult to see?

3   Work with a partner. Take turns asking and answering the questions in Exercise 2.

Speaking model

You are going to learn about using the present progressive tense for changes over time, giving reasons for and against something, and pronouncing contractions in present progressive statements. You are then going to use these to talk about a trend in a city you know well.

A Analyze

1 Complete the talk below with the phrases in the box.

> One advantage is that that the new buildings are safe
> the rents in my city are becoming
> but in the end I'm against this trend
> builders are destroying historic buildings

One way that my city is changing is that [1]_____ in the downtown area and building modern ones in their place. This trend has both advantages and disadvantages. [2]_____ and attractive. Also, they make the city better for tourists and businesses. However, there are also serious disadvantages. First, because of the new buildings, [3]_____ more and more expensive. Many poor people have to move because they can't afford the rents in the new buildings. Another disadvantage is traffic. The new buildings are usually enormous, with many apartments with more people. As a result, there are more and more drivers on the streets, and it's getting harder and harder to find parking. I support making the city safe and beautiful, [4]_____. I think it's unfair that poor people are losing their homes.

2 The talk above has the following parts. Put the parts in the order they are mentioned.

___ advantages   ___ speaker's opinion   ___ trend   ___ disadvantages

B Discuss

Work with a partner. Answer the questions.

1 How many advantages does the speaker mention? How many disadvantages?

2 What are some more advantages or disadvantages of destroying historic buildings and putting up modern ones?

3 Is this trend also happening in your city? Is it a good thing or a bad thing, in your opinion? Why?

Grammar

The present progressive tense for changes over time

The present progressive tense is used to talk about actions happening now.

What are you working on?   *I am studying Chemistry at university.*

You can also use it with double adjectives or adverbs to talk about changes that are happening over a period of time.

Subject + *is/are* **+ verb (-ing) +** *more and more* **+ adjective/adverb**

The city is getting more and more crowded.

Subject + *is/are* **+ verb (-ing) + adjective/adverb +** *and* **+ adjective/adverb**

Wallscapes are getting bigger and bigger.

Notice that the comparative adjective is repeated two times.

Adjective	Comparative form	Double comparative adjective
big	*bigger*	*bigger and bigger*
crowded	*more crowded*	*more and more crowded*

1 Complete the sentences with the present progressive form.

1 The population of Los Angeles _____ (grow).

2 I _____ (work) as an intern for an advertising company for two weeks.

3 My friend _____ (look) for a new apartment downtown.

4 You can turn off the TV. We _____ (not/watch) it.

5 I want to visit Germany so I _____ (study) German at the moment.

2 Put the following adjectives into their double comparative adjective form.

1	bad	*worse and worse*	6	common	_____
2	small	*smaller and smaller*	7	fast	_____
3	expensive	_____	8	difficult	_____
4	good	_____	9	tall	_____
5	cheap	_____	10	popular	_____

3 Make sentences with the words below. Use the present progressive form.

1 In Los Angeles, public transportation / get / good

In Los Angeles, public transportation is getting better and better.

2 Buildings / get / tall

3 Many cities / become / crowded

4 The world's population / grow / fast

5 Life in most cities / get / expensive

Speaking skill

Sometimes people have strong opinions for or against a plan, idea, or situation. When you express a strong opinion, it is a good idea to give reasons to support it.

Giving reasons for something

(Subject) (*be*) *for* + verb -ing	(Subject) + *support* + verb -ing
+ noun	+ noun

I am for planting more trees in my city **because** they make the city beautiful.

Most people support the new law **because** it is fair.

Giving reasons against something

(Subject) (*be*) *against* + verb -ing
+ noun

(Subject) + (*doesn't* /*don't*) *support* + verb -ing
+ noun

Many people are against the new light rail project **because** it costs too much.

I don't support building tall buildings **because** they hide the sun and make the streets dark.

1 **4.5 Listen and complete the sentences with the missing expressions.**

1 I _____ a new city tax because taxes are already very high.

2 I'm _____ people using cell phones while driving because it isn't safe.

3 In my city, most people are _____ saving water because we don't have enough rain.

4 I _____ recycling because it's good for the environment.

5 My neighbor is _____ billboards because he thinks they're a kind of pollution.

6 Almost everybody is _____ the new Metro system because there isn't enough parking downtown.

2 **Work with a partner. Take turns giving your opinion about the ideas.**

1 Our city is planning to close all the libraries on weekends to save money.

2 Some cities don't allow cars in the downtown area. People have to park outside the downtown area and take public transportation to the center.

3 Our city is spending 3 million dollars to plant thousands of trees in public places.

4 Our city wants to spend ten million dollars on a new metro system. People can travel to the city center faster, but it will take four years to complete.

Pronunciation for speaking

Pronouncing contractions in the present progressive

All forms of be are usually contracted in the present progressive tense.

Affirmative		Negative	
I'm	it's	I'm not	it's not or it isn't
you're	we're	you're not or you aren't	we're not or we aren't
he's	they're	he's not or he isn't	they're not or they aren't
she's		she's not or she isn't	

Word stress in the present progressive

Stress the participle (-ing word) in affirmative statements.
Stress not + participle in negative statements.

I'm **go**ing. I'm **not go**ing.

She's **sleep**ing. She's **not sleep**ing. / She **isn't sleep**ing.

1 🎧 4.6 Listen and complete the sentences with the contracted form.

1 _____ standing at the corner of 5th and Main.

2 _____ not raining now.

3 She _____ driving to work today.

4 _____ putting up an enormous wallscape.

5 _____ planning to move to Istanbul.

6 _____ living in an apartment downtown.

7 _____ not meeting with the teacher today.

8 They _____ listening to the speaker.

2 Underline the contractions in the conversation below. Then read the conversation with a partner. Focus on contractions and correct word stress.

Henry: The traffic in my city is getting worse and worse. It's a big problem for my brother. He's working in a tourist office downtown. Sometimes it takes him 40 minutes to drive 2 kilometers.

Roberto: Wow. Is the city doing anything to improve the situation?

Henry: Yes. They're planning to create a "park-and-ride" system. The idea is that you can park your car outside the downtown area and take a bus to the center.

Henry: I'm all for that.

Roberto: Me too. But the disadvantage is that it's going to take five years to finish it.

Henry: I think the situation will be better in five years.

Roberto: Yes, I guess you're right.

Speaking task

Talk about a trend that is happening in a city.

Brainstorm

Read the trends below. Think of changes that are happening to your city or a city you know well. Add two more trends to the list. Decide if you are for or against each trend and give a reason.

More and more people are moving to cities. I'm against this because …

1 More and more people are moving to cities.
2 Rents are rising higher and higher.
3 The city is planting more trees / building more parks.
4 Builders are replacing historic buildings with modern ones.
5 More outdoor advertising is appearing.
6 The city is becoming "smarter."
7 _____
8 _____

Plan

Look back at your ideas in the Brainstorm and select one trend to talk about. Then plan a short talk. Use the speaking model on page 74 to help you. Include the following in your plan:

- present progressive statements for showing changes over time
- advantages and disadvantages
- your opinion and reasons why you are for or against the trend
- vocabulary from Unit 4

Speak

Practice your presentation. Pay attention to your pronunciation of contractions and word stress in present progressive statements.

Share

Form a group. Take turns giving your talks and giving feedback.

Reflect

Look back at the ideas presented in the unit and answer the question "How are cities changing?" With a group, discuss three trends you learned about in this unit.

Review

Wordlist

MACMILLAN DICTIONARY

Vocabulary preview

crowded (adj)*	mixed (adj)**	space (n)***
differences (n)***	outdoor (adj)*	system (n)***
grow (v)***	pollution (n)***	top (n)***
huge (adj)***	product (n)***	trend (n)***
level (n)***	public (adj)***	

Vocabulary development

business (n)***	increase (v) ***	popular (adj)***
downtown (adj)	neighborhood (n)**	tourists (n)***
historic (adj)**	parking (n)*	

Academic words

area (n)***	document (n)***	equipment (n)***
channel (n)***	enormous (adj.)***	obvious (adj)***

Academic words review

Complete the sentences with the words in the box.

biology   document   enormous   interview   site

1 My whole area looks like a construction _____ at the moment.
2 I study _____ at California State. I'm planning to become a scientist.
3 I always get very nervous before a job _____.
4 What kinds of _____ do I need to print out? The map and the invitation?
5 I live in an _____ apartment building on the 15th floor.

Unit review

Listening 1		I can listen for corrections.
Listening 2		I can listen for advantages and disadvantages.
Vocabulary		I can use words to describe cities.
Grammar		I can use the present progressive for changes over time.
Speaking		I can give reasons for or against something.
Pronunciation		I can use contractions with *be*.

Customs around the world

Discussion point

Study the infographic and answer the questions.

1 In which country is it polite to leave a little food on your plate at the end of a meal?

2 In which country should you not give the host yellow or red flowers?

3 Which customs are similar in your country?

Greetings

In Maori, New Zealand, some people greet by pressing their foreheads together.

It is common in India for younger people to touch older people's feet to show respect.

Meals

In Colombia, don't begin eating until host says "Buen Provecho" ("Enjoy your meal").

It's polite to leave a little food on your plate at the end of a meal in Italy.

Gift-giving

When invited to a Russian home, give the host chocolates and dessert items.

When invited to a Mexican home, give the host flowers; don't give yellow or red flowers.

VIDEO

FINISHING SCHOOL

Before you watch

Which skills and customs are important to know when you meet business people (**B**) and friends (**F**) from another country? Write **B** or **F**. Some may have more than one answer.

be informal	_____	know about etiquette	_____
be polite	_B & F_	be on time for meetings	_____
eat in the correct way	_____	learn their customs	_____
give a gift	_____	shake hands when you meet	_____

UNIT AIMS

LISTENING 1 Listening for explanations and examples
LISTENING 2 Listening for the main ideas of a lecture
STUDY SKILL Slide presentations

VOCABULARY Words for customs and traditions
GRAMMAR Giving advice
SPEAKING Introducing a talk

A family dinner in China.

While you watch

Watch the video. Choose the correct option to complete each sentence.

The finishing school teaches students …

1 subjects **usually / not usually** taught at high school.

2 **bad / good** behavior.

3 to eat with a **knife and fork / chopsticks**.

4 how to **talk / serve food** at a dinner party.

5 **more / less** international etiquette and protocol.

6 **to work in your family business / to be an international business woman**.

After you watch

Work with a partner. Discuss the questions.

1 Would you like to go to a finishing school? Why / Why not?

   Yes, I think I would because …

   No, I wouldn't because …

2 Why should you learn about customs and traditions in other countries?

   It's important because …

3 What other subjects are important to learn at school?

   [Economics] is important because …

   It would be a good idea to teach … because …

Japanese customs

A Vocabulary preview

1 Match the words in bold with the correct definition.

1	**greeting** (n)	a	things that people do that are traditional or usual
2	**customs** (n)	b	feeling a little worried or scared
3	**nervous** (adj)	c	words or actions you use to show that someone is important
4	**respect** (n)		
5	**title** (n)	d	something that you say or do when you meet someone
6	**luck** (n)	e	a person whose house you visit for dinner or a party
7	**host** (n)	f	a word before someone's name like 'Doctor' or 'Mrs.'
8	**upset** (v)	g	to make someone unhappy or angry
		h	success or failure by chance

2 Complete each sentence with a word in bold from Exercise 1.

1 I always address my teachers with their title and family name to show them _____.

2 The main _____ in my country when you meet someone is 'Mahaba'.

3 Most of the _____ in my country are difficult to understand for foreign visitors.

4 I am always very _____ when I have to take an English test.

5 I hope to have the _____ of Dr. or Prof. in the future.

6 I don't want to _____ my parents by getting bad grades.

7 It is normal in my country to give chocolates to the _____ if you have dinner at their house.

8 In my country, the number 13 brings bad _____.

3 Which of the statements above are true for you?

B Before you listen

1 Write one custom from your country for each topic below.

Greetings	Meals	Gift-giving
shake hands	leave some food on the plate	don't give white flowers

2 Do you know a custom from another country? Discuss your ideas with your partner.

C Global listening

1 🎧 **5.1** Listen to *Japanese customs*. Choose the correct column for each custom on the left.

	Greetings	Meals	Gift-giving
bow to show respect	☐	☐	☐
use titles with people's names	☐	☐	☐
thank people for food	☐	☐	☐
don't stand chopsticks up in a bowl	☐	☐	☐
use both hands	☐	☐	☐

2 🎧 **5.1** Listen to *Japanese customs* again and choose the correct option to complete the sentences.

1 Donna is nervous because she …

 a doesn't like Japanese food.

 b doesn't know anything about Japan.

 c will have a Japanese exchange student as a guest.

2 When you meet people in a high position, it's polite to bow …

 a more quickly. b lower and longer. c while smiling.

3 People say, "Thank you for the food." …

 a during a meal. b at the end of a meal.

 c at the beginning of a meal.

4 People say, "It's just a small thing" when …

 a they give a gift. b they receive a gift. c open a gift.

5 It's considered unlucky to give …

 a two cakes. b five flowers. c four or nine of anything.

Listening for explanations and examples

D Close listening

Speakers often give an explanation or example to make their ideas clearer and easier to understand. Recognizing the signals a speaker uses to introduce an explanation or example will improve your comprehension. You can use these words and phrases:

Explanation	**Example**
which/that means …, in other words … meaning that …	*like, …, such as …, for example …, a few examples are …*

1 🎧 **5.2** Listen to excerpts from *Japanese Customs* and complete the sentences below.

1 Mainly about some of the customs, _____ greetings, table manners, gift giving …

2 It's polite to bow a little lower to people in a higher position, _____ officials or managers.

3 The Japanese are quite formal, so it's normal to add *-san* after a person's family name, _____, Suzuki-*san*.

4 Before you begin a meal, it's polite to say *Itadakimasu*. _____ 'thank you for the food'.

5 When you give a gift, it's normal to say that it's *tsumaranai mono*, _____ 'it's just a small thing'.

2 Write the word *explanation* or *example* next to each answer in Exercise 2.

E Critical thinking

Discuss the questions.

1 Which Japanese customs are similar to customs in your county? Which are different?

   The custom of … is similar/different in my country.

2 What custom in your country is important or useful for foreign visitors to know about?

   One useful custom to know about is …

3 Is it important to learn about other countries' customs and traditions? Why / Why not?

   I think it is/isn't important to learn about customs in other countries because …

Pronunciation for listening

Weak forms

In Unit 4, you studied reduced forms and how to pronounce the schwa sound /ə/.

Weak forms also occur with the words *a,* and *an*. We use *a* before consonant sounds and *an* before vowel sounds. The weak forms of *a* and *an* use the schwa sound /ə/.

The words *there's* and *there are* are often pronounced in their weak form.

Note: We use the word *there* in its strong form when we talk about a place or location or when we are confirming or contrasting information with *there is* or *there are*.

A: *Where's my jacket?*   B: *Over there.*

1 **5.3** Listen, notice and underline the schwa sound /ə/ in *a, an,* or *there* in each sentence.

1   I'm a bit nervous.
2   It's a fascinating country.
3   Do Japanese people use titles a lot?
4   Well, before you begin a meal, it's polite to say *Itadakimasu*.
5   Actually, there are lots of important gift-giving customs.
6   You're definitely an expert on Japanese customs.
7   You should always present a gift with both hands.
8   That means it's just a small thing.

2 **5.4** Listen and mark the underlined words with *S* (Strong form) or *W* (Weak form).

1 A: Where's my laptop?
   B: It's over [1] there.
2 A: [2] There's a big art exhibition in New York.
   B: Yes, there is. I went [3] there last week.
3 A: I have [4] a big presentation tomorrow.
   B: Good luck! I'm sure it will go well.
4 A: My city has [5] an excellent Italian restaurant downtown.
   B: Great! Let's go [6] there next week.

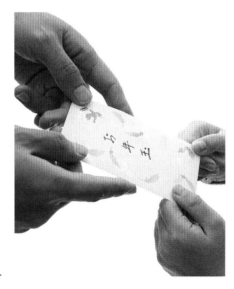

Culture corner

A Vocabulary preview

1 Match the words in bold with the correct definition.

1	**celebrate** (v)	a	to change, grow, or become more successful over time
2	**develop** (v)	b	people living together in a particular country or area
3	**purpose** (n)	c	to do something fun to show that an event or occasion is special
4	**society** (n)	d	the aim or goal of a person, thing, or action
5	**generation** (n)		
6	**particular** (adj)	e	a period of the year with different weather, e.g. summer
7	**season** (n)	f	things that you do often or regularly
8	**habits** (n)	g	about one specific person or thing
		h	a group of people who are born and live at around the same time

2 Complete the sentences with the words in bold from Exercise 1.

a   How do you usually _____ your birthday?

b   Do you think one _____ of education is to learn about different cultures?

c   What kinds of activities help you _____ your English skills the most?

d   In your country, is _____ changing a lot these days?

e   What _____ should you have to be a successful student?

f   What is your favorite _____? Personally, I like winter.

g   Is there a _____ holiday that you love the most?

h   In what ways is your _____ different from your parents'?

3 Ask and answer the questions in Exercise 2 with a partner.

B Before you listen

Activating prior knowledge

Work with a partner. Discuss the questions.

1   Do you enjoy learning about other countries' customs? Why?

I (don't) enjoy … because …

2   Are traditional customs an important part of life in your country?

I (don't) think customs are important in my country because …

3   Are there any customs in your country that foreign visitors may find strange?

One strange custom in my country is …

C Global listening

At the beginning of a lecture or presentation the speaker usually tells you what the main topics are and in what order they will come. If you listen carefully for these signal words and phrases for the main topics, it will be easier to follow the lecture or presentation and take notes.

main topics: *talk about, look at, consider, cover*

order: *first, then, next, finally, last*

Listening for the main ideas of a talk

1 🎧 5.5 Listen to the first part of *Culture corner*. Choose the words that you hear.

1	Today	✓	4	First	___	7	Then	___
2	Tomorrow	___	5	Next	___	8	Number three	___
3	One	___	6	Second	___	9	Finally	___

2 🎧 5.5 Listen again to the first part of *Culture corner*. Number the topics in the order you hear them.

CUSTOMS IN SOCIETY

_____ I'll explain how customs develop

_____ I'll talk about the purpose of customs

_____ we'll consider the future of customs

_____ we'll look at the meaning of customs

Listening for details

D Close listening

🎧 **5.6** Listen to the rest of the presentation. Complete the slides with the correct information. Use one word or number for each blank.

WHAT ARE CUSTOMS?

The ^{1}_____ way people do something
The common practices in a community:
a country, ^{2} a_____ or an organization
Includes greetings, gift-giving, weddings and meals

WHERE DO CUSTOMS COME FROM?

Develop from daily ^{3}_____ and activities
Involve different areas of life:
food, ^{4}_____, clothing, language, etc.
Over many years, people repeat these and they become customs

THE PURPOSE OF CUSTOMS

Customs have ^{5}_____ main purposes:
1   accepted rules of our social life
2   give people feeling of comfort and ^{6}_____
3   keep our culture alive

THE FUTURE OF CUSTOMS

Normally stronger in older, more traditional societies
Many traditional societies are becoming more ^{7}_____ and developed.
People listen to the same music, watch the same movies
Sounds negative, but it means customs are becoming more ^{8}_____.

E Critical thinking

Discuss the questions.

1   Explain three different customs in your country.
    In my country, people usually …

2   Do you think customs are important? Why?
    I think customs are/aren't very important because …

3   How can we keep customs alive in a modern world?
    I think we can keep customs alive with / by + verb (-ing) …

Study skills   Slide presentations

- Use large text: at least 28 point.
- Introduce new slides from the same direction.
- Use only one slide for every two minutes of the talk.
- Only use animations, sound effects, or strange graphics if they are necessary.
- If you use video clips, keep these very short (under 2–3 minutes).

© Stella Cottrell (2013)

GLOSSARY

clip (n) a short part of a video
graphic (n) a type of drawing
slide (n) a single page of a presentation
sound effects (n) the recorded sound in a movie, TV program, or presentation

1 Read the study skills box. Choose *T* (True) or *F* (False).

1 If you want to put a lot of information on your slide, you should use 16-point font.

True   False

2 If you introduce slide 1 from the left, you should also introduce slide 2 from the left.

True   False

3 If your talk is ten minutes long, you should use six slides.

True   False

4 If your talk is 15 minutes long, you should use a five-minute video.

True   False

2 Work with a partner. Take turns introducing the slides from a talk about customs in Spain. Use the phrases from the Useful phrases box.

Useful phrases

As you can see...
on this slide,
on the next slide,
here,

GREETINGS IN SPAIN

Polite to shake hands with all people: men, women, children

ATTITUDES TO TIME IN SPAIN

OK to be late for social events
Visiting friend's home for dinner—not common to arrive early

GIFT-GIVING IN SPAIN

When visiting someone's home—bring a gift!
Box of chocolates or dessert
Not common to give flowers

Vocabulary development

Words for customs and traditions

1 Match the words from the box with the correct meaning.

> acceptable   celebration   common   guest
> invitation   polite   receive   wedding

1 _____ (adj) to behave towards other people in a pleasant way
2 _____ (n) to be fine or good enough for a particular situation
3 _____ (n) a party for a birthday or a public holiday
4 _____ (adj) happening all the time
5 _____ (n) an offer from someone to do something together
6 _____ (n) someone who you have asked to your home
7 _____ (n) a ceremony in which two people get married
8 _____ (v) to get something from someone, like a gift

2 Complete the sentences with the words from Exercise 1.

1 It is _____ for many people in my country to drink tea in the afternoon.
2 New Year's Eve is an important _____ in my country.
3 In my country, money is an _____ gift for a birthday.
4 When I meet a friend I'm always on time because I think it's not _____ to be late.
5 When I am a _____ in someone's home, I always bring a gift.
6 Children usually _____ money from their parents at New Year.
7 In my country, when people get married, there are about 300 people at the _____.
8 We send an _____ to everyone we know when we have a party.

3 Complete the text about Greek weddings with words from Exercise 1.

In Greece, some people follow a lot of traditions when they get married. When a man asks a woman to marry him, it is [1]_____ for the couple to exchange rings. This is a formal occasion, so people wear smart suits and dresses. The couple then set the date for the [2]_____. Some dates are not [3]_____ for a wedding because they are considered unlucky. For example the first two weeks of August. The wedding [4]_____ can take an hour and the couple hold a candle and drink from the same cup. Then the party begins—the couple invite all of their friends and relatives to the celebration. There are usually many people there, because it is considered impolite to refuse a wedding [5]_____. People eat special food, and there is a lot of dancing. When the party is over, each [6]_____ is given a small bag of almonds or sweets to take home.

Academic words

1 Match the words in bold with the correct definition.

1 **contact** (v)   a a set of clothes that you wear for a special occasion
2 **expert** (n)   b traditional in idea or style
3 **attitude** (n)   c to get in touch or communicate with someone
4 **costume** (n)   d someone's opinions or feelings about something
5 **license** (n)   e someone who knows a lot about a subject or topic
6 **classical** (adj)   f a document or card that allows you to do something, like drive a car

2 Complete each sentence with a word in bold from Exercise 1.

1 In your country, do people wear a traditional _____ when they get married?
2 Do you enjoy listening to _____ music? Why / Why not?
3 What must you do to get a driving _____ in your country?
4 Do you have friends you can _____ in other countries when you travel?
5 Are you an _____ on the culture and customs in your country?
6 What is your _____ to time? Do you mind if people are late for a meeting?

3 Work with a partner. Answer the questions in Exercise 2 and explain your answers.

In my country, people wear ... when they get married.

Speaking model

You are going to learn about giving advice, asking for ideas and examples, and pronouncing syllable stress. You are then going to give advice about cultural customs in a short talk.

A Analyze

Hello, I'm Helge. Welcome to my short presentation on customs. Today, I'll cover three customs in Germany that will be very useful when you visit. First, I'll talk about greetings and how to address people, then I'll move onto attitudes to time in society and finally, I'll explain a custom about gift-giving. To begin with, it is polite to call people by their surname in Germany. This is very common in the workplace with people you know well, like your colleagues, and people you don't know well, such as customers. Next, it is not a good idea to be late. It is considered rude to arrive late to a social event or meeting so you should be on time for everything. Finally, it is a good idea to bring a gift when you are invited to a friend or colleague's house. In Germany, people normally give chocolates as a present. It's not so common to give flowers.

1 Put the topics in the order they are mentioned.

___ gift-giving   ___ greetings   ___ attitudes to time

2 Underline the six phrases the speaker uses to give advice. What type of word follows the phrases? The first one has been done for you.

3 Complete each sentence with the correct advice about German customs.

1 You are in Germany and you meet a colleague you know well. You should call them …

    a   by their first name

    b   by their surname

    c   by their first name and surname

2 You are invited to a friend's home for dinner. They tell you to come at 8:00 p.m. You should …

    a   arrive at 7:30 p.m.   b   arrive at 8:00 p.m.   c   arrive at 8:30 p.m.

3 You want to bring a gift when you visit your friend's home. You should bring …

    a   some flowers   b   a loaf of bread   c   chocolates

B Discuss

Which customs in Germany are similar and different to those in your country?

Grammar

Giving advice

We can give advice and make suggestions with the adjective expression:

It is + adjective + infinitive form

It is common to give chocolates.

We can also use the modal verb *should / shouldn't*.

should / shouldn't + base form of infinitive verb

You should arrive on time for business meetings. You shouldn't bring white flowers when visiting someone's home.

Notice which adjective expressions and modal verbs have a similar meaning:

It is + adjective + to + verb		modal verb
It is a good idea to …	=	*should*
It is polite to …	=	*should*
It is not a good idea to …	=	*shouldn't / should not*
It is impolite/rude to …	=	*shouldn't / should not*

1 Complete the sentences with *should* and a verb from the box.

> be   give   remove   say   take   wrap

1 Gift-giving is very important in Turkey so you _____ a gift when visiting a new home.

2 Before starting a meal in France, you _____ 'bon appétit' which means 'enjoy your meal.'

3 You _____ on time for meetings in Germany.

4 In Brazil you _____ not _____ a gift with black or purple paper as those colors are for funerals.

5 In many countries you _____ your hat when entering a building.

6 In China, you should _____ your business card with both hands.

2 Look at the Japanese cultural *Do's* and *Don'ts* below. Practice with a partner making sentences using the phrases in the Grammar box.

Do	**Don't**
greet the oldest person first	wrap gifts in white paper
bring your host a gift	give an even number of flowers
arrive on time for a meeting	talk loudly on your phone on a train
remove your shoes in a home	leave a tip in a restaurant

It is polite to greet the oldest person first.

Speaking skill

It is important to make a good introduction when giving a talk. Your introduction should ...

- greet and welcome people
- introduce yourself
- state the purpose or topic of your talk
- outline the structure of your talk.

1 Match the purposes on the left with the phrases on the right.

1 Greet and welcome people   a *Today, I'd like to talk about ...*

2 Introduce yourself   b *My talk is divided into three parts. First, ... Next, ... Finally, ...*

3 State the topic of your talk

4 Outline the structure of   c *My name is ...*
  your talk   d *Good morning everyone. I'm happy to see you all.*

2 Put the phrases from Exercise 1 into the introduction for the presentation *Customs in Turkey*. Include *first, next* and *finally*.

Customs in Turkey

Good morning everyone. _____ you all. _____ Mehmet. _____ about customs in Turkey. _____ three parts. _____, I will talk about greetings, and tell you how to address people in my country. _____, I will discuss the topic of gift giving, including acceptable gifts to give to people. _____, I will give you advice on the best way to work with people from my country.

3 Choose a country. Think of three topics you can talk about from the box below. Then, make an introduction to your partner.

| Gift giving | Greetings | Attitudes to time | Dining & Meals | Weddings |

_____

_____

_____

_____

_____

_____

_____

Pronunciation for speaking

Pronouncing syllable stress

In multi-syllable words, the stress always falls on **one** of the syllables.

Most two-syllable nouns and adjectives have the stress on the **first** syllable:

customs   **ques**tions   **greet**ings   **ner**vous

Many two-syllable verbs have the stress on the **second** syllable

ex**plain**   in**clude**   re**peat**   ex**ist**

The word ending can often be a good guide:

Words ending in -er, -ly: Stress the first syllable
= **eas**ier   **to**tally

Words ending in -sion, -tion: Stress the second to last syllable
= tele**vis**ion   re**la**tion

Words ending in -cy, -ty, -phy, -gy: Stress the third from last syllable
= so**ci**ety   **En**ergy

1 🎧 5.7 Listen and underline the stressed syllables. Check your answers in a dictionary. Then listen again and repeat.

1	common	5	normally
2	daily	6	traditions
3	begin	7	community
4	accept	8	unlucky

2 Write the words from the box in the correct column according to their stress pattern. Use a dictionary to help you.

agree   celebrate   common   cultural   decide
family   formal   generation   including   information
invite   normal   position   remember   understanding

Oo	oO	Ooo	oOo	ooOo

3 Work with a partner. Say the words and check each other's pronunciation of word stress.

Speaking task

Give a small talk about customs and traditions in a country.

Brainstorm

Read the information in the chart about customs in three countries on page 188. Choose one country and research one custom for each of the topics.

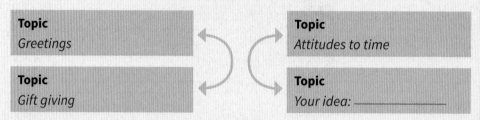

Topic	**Topic**
Greetings	*Attitudes to time*

Topic	**Topic**
Gift giving	*Your idea:* _____

Plan

Make notes for a small talk which gives advice about three customs in the country that you chose. Write the introduction using the phrases from page 93 and give advice about customs using the phrases from page 90.

> *Country:* _____
>
> *Introduction:*_____
>
> _____
>
> _____
>
> _____
>
> _____
>
> _____.
>
> | *Topic* | *Custom* |
> |---|---|
> | *Greetings* | _____ |
> | *Attitudes to time* | _____ |
> | *Gift giving* | _____ |

Speak

Present your talk to a partner. Notice your pronunciation of multi-syllable words. Make notes of the new customs you learn about.

Share

Work with a new partner. Share the information you learned from your partner.

Reflect

Using the information you learned throughout the unit, answer the questions.

1   What customs from other countries do you find most interesting?
2   Why is it important for a country to have customs?
3   Are customs becoming more international? Why / Why not?

Review

Wordlist

MACMILLAN DICTIONARY

Vocabulary preview

celebrate (v)***	host (n) **	season (n)***
customs (n)*	luck (n)**	society (n)***
develop (v)***	nervous (adj)**	title (n) ***
generation (n)***	particular (adj)***	upset (v)**
greeting (n) ***	purpose (n)***	
habits (n)***	respect (n)***	

Vocabulary development

acceptable (adj) **	guest (n)***	receive (v)***
celebration (n)***	invitation (n)***	wedding (n) ***
common (adj)***	polite (adj)***	

Academic words

attitude (n)***	contact (v)***	expert (n)***
classical (adj)**	costume (n)*	license (n)***

Academic words review

Complete the sentences with the words in the box.

attitude	classical	design	similar	label

1 She has a positive _____ and is open to different cultures and customs.
2 Some countries have _____ ways of greeting people but in some places, greetings are very different.
3 I am studying _____ literature from many different countries.
4 Please _____ the room using traditional styles, patterns, and shapes.
5 Can you give me a sticky _____ for my file?

Unit review

Listening 1	I can listen for explanations and examples.
Listening 2	I can listen for the main ideas of a lecture.
Vocabulary	I can use words for customs and traditions.
Grammar	I can give advice.
Speaking	I can introduce a talk.
Pronunciation	I can pronounce syllable stress

A balanced diet

Discussion point

Study the infographic and answer the questions.

1 Compare your diet to the recommendations. How is your diet similar? How is it different?

   I don't eat dairy products. I eat more meat.

2 Add one more type of food to each group.

3 Are there any foods in the chart that are not healthy, in your opinion?

   I think bread is not healthy because …

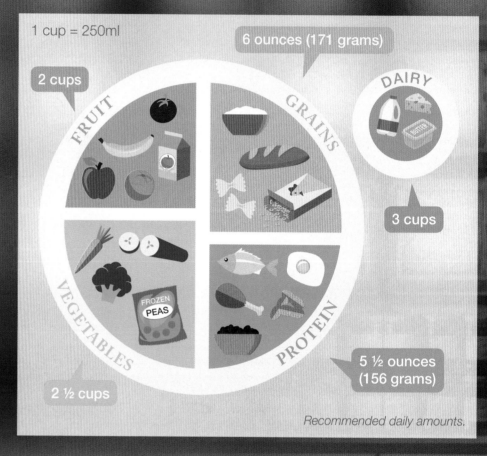

1 cup = 250ml

2 cups — FRUIT

6 ounces (171 grams) — GRAINS

DAIRY — 3 cups

VEGETABLES — 2 ½ cups

FROZEN PEAS

PROTEIN — 5 ½ ounces (156 grams)

Recommended daily amounts.

VIDEO

MOON CAKES

Before you watch

Work with a partner. Do you agree with these sentences? Why? / Why not?

1 Cakes filled with sugar and other sweet things have lots of calories.

2 Sweets and cakes can only taste delicious if they have lots of sugar.

3 It is better for your health to eat ingredients like fruit, nuts, and seeds.

UNIT AIMS

LISTENING 1 Listening for opinions
LISTENING 2 Listening for steps in a process
STUDY SKILL Active and passive learning

VOCABULARY Sequencers
GRAMMAR Present passive
SPEAKING Explanation signals

A shop owner in Turkey.

While you watch

Read the sentences and predict the correct answer. Watch the video. Check your answers.

1 People buy mooncakes to eat in the autumn for **birthdays / for a festival**.

2 Traditional mooncakes usually have lots of **colors / sugar and calories**.

3 In the video you can see a cake with an egg yolk which represents **the moon / autumn**.

4 "Health-conscious people" means people who like a **balanced diet / unhealthy food**.

5 The main idea of the video is that the new mooncakes **are not popular with customers / use healthy ingredients**.

After you watch

Work with a partner. Discuss the questions.

1 Do you prefer sweet or savory foods? Why / Why not?

   I prefer sweet / savory foods because …

2 Do you have pasties, or cakes, with similar ingredients to the mooncake in your country?

   In my country, we have …

3 What food do you eat during festivals and celebrations?

   Normally, we eat …

Lab burger

A Vocabulary preview

1 Match the words in bold with the correct definition.

1	**laboratory** (n)	a	a new event that changes a situation
2	**development** (n)	b	information that helps us understand a situation or problem
3	**disgusting** (adj)		
4	**background** (n)	c	a place where people do scientific or medical researc
5	**beef** (n)	d	tasting very bad
6	**process** (n)	e	tasting very good
7	**tasty** (adj)	f	a group of actions that happen in order and end with particular result
8	**products** (n)		
		g	the meat from a cow
		h	things that people make or buy

2 Complete the sentences with words in bold from Exercise 1.

1 I want to be a scientist and work in a _____ in the future.

2 I like most vegetables, but I hate broccoli. I think it's _____.

3 In my opinion, the electric car is the most important _____ of the 21st century so far.

4 I often shop online for personal _____ like clothes and shoes.

5 Some people don't like olives, but I think they're very _____.

6 I know how to make coffee. It's a simple _____, with just two or three steps.

7 I'm a vegetarian, so I don't eat meat such as _____.

8 I always use the internet to find _____ information on a new topic.

3 Work with a partner. Which of the sentences in Exercise 2 are true for you?

B Before you listen

Activating prior knowledge

Work with a partner. Discuss the questions.

1 What are some popular meat dishes in your country?

... is a very popular meat dish in my country.

2 Some people don't eat meat. What reasons do they give?

Some people don't eat meat because ...

3 Is it possible to make a beef burger in a laboratory?

C Global listening

1 🎧 **6.1** Listen to the conversation. Put the topics in the order they are discussed.

Listening for main ideas

___ disadvantages of lab-grown beef

_1_ background about the world's population

___ shopping for meat in the future

___ reasons why we can't continue to eat beef from cows

___ the process of making meat in a lab

Listening for opinions

> Facts are true statements that you can prove. Facts do not change from person to person. For example, Yasmin says "*Cows need a huge amount of space to grow*." We can look on the Internet to learn if this statement is correct.
>
> On the other hand, an opinion is something a person believes. Different people can have different opinions. To recognize an opinion, listen for phrases like these:
>
> *I think …   I believe …   In my opinion …   I agree/disagree.*

2 🎧 **6.1** Listen again. Which speaker expresses the following opinions? Write the name of the person in the box below next to the opinion.

Marcus   Yasmin   Flora

1 Lab-grown beef is an amazing development.	
2 Lab-grown meat is disgusting.	
3 Lab-grown meat is not disgusting.	
4 The lower cost is a huge benefit.	

A lab-grown beef burger

Listening for details

D Close listening

1 🔊 **6.2** Listen again to part of the conversation. Which problems with eating farm-raised beef does Yasmin mention? Choose three correct answers.

1 ___ Cows need a lot of space and water.

2 ___ Cows create pollution.

3 ___ Eating beef is not healthy.

4 ___ Killing animals for food isn't kind.

2 🔊 **6.3** Listen again to the steps in preparing lab-grown meat. Complete each sentence with a word from the box.

| cells | color | cook | grow | hamburger |

1 Scientists take muscle _____ from a living cow.

2 They allow the cells to _____ and divide in the lab.

3 They use the cells to make a _____.

4 They add eggs, breadcrumbs, and vegetable juice to give the meat _____.

5 They _____ the hamburger.

3 🔊 **6.4** Listen to the last part of the conversation. Which disadvantages of lab-grown beef are mentioned? Choose two correct answers.

1 The technology is new.

2 Some people think lab-grown beef is disgusting.

3 It will be very expensive to produce.

E Critical thinking

Discuss the questions.

1 Look at the table in Exercise 2 on page 101. Do you agree more with Yasmin or Flora's opinion about the lab-grown hamburger?

I agree with Yasmin/Flora that lab-grown beef is ...

2 Imagine it is 15 years from now. You bring home lab-grown beef to make your family's dinner. What will they say?

I think my family will say ...

3 Is making food in a laboratory the future of food production?

Yes, I think making food in a lab is the future of food production because ...
No, I don't think making food in a lab is the future of food production because ...

Active and passive learning

Traditional learning can be quite passive. The teacher talks and the students listen and perhaps take notes. Later they repeat the information on a test. Active learning is very different. Lessons are interactive, with students asking questions, offering ideas, and working together. Teachers expect students to think critically and be responsible for their own learning.

1 Match the characteristics of passive and active learners.

Passive learning	Active learning
1 You wait for the professor to give you directions and information.	a You make an effort to find the meaning of what you learn, so your understanding is better.
2 You repeat information without understanding it.	b You think, analyze, and reflect on the information your professor provided.
3 You write down what the professor says, but you don't think about it later.	c You ask questions and look for ways to become more involved in what you are learning.
4 You don't think about ways to use what you learn in your own life.	d You look for ways to apply what you are learning to situations in your life.

© Stella Cottrell (2013)

2 Look at the sentences below. Which are characteristics of a passive learner and active learner? Write P (Passive learner) or A (Active learner) next to each sentence.

1 "I should copy this out".

2 "Evaluate your own work".

3 "Set yourself questions to answer later".

4 "Strange, I've finished and I don't remember a thing".

3 Work with a partner. Use the information in Exercises 1 and 2. Are you an active or passive learner? If you are passive, what steps can you take to become more active?

Let's concentrate on orange juice

A Vocabulary preview

1 Read the sentences. Match the words in bold with the correct definition.

1 Professor Smith's **lecture** about the latest developments in growing food was very interesting.

2 I don't know how to use the washing machine in my new apartment. Can you **explain** it to me?

3 To make fresh orange juice, you need to cut the oranges and then **squeeze** out the juice.

4 The best way to **protect** your skin from the hot sun is to wear a hat and long sleeves.

5 If you want to have a healthy **heart**, get plenty of exercise and don't smoke.

6 In many cultures, it is polite to **remove** your shoes before you enter someone's house.

a _____ (v) to tell or show so that something will be easier to understand

b _____ (v) to press hard, for example to remove water from something

c _____ (n) a long talk about a topic, especially at a university

d _____ (v) to take off or take away

e _____ (n) the part of your body that sends blood to all the other parts

f _____ (v) to keep someone or something safe from harm or damage

2 Work with a partner. Take turns reading and answering the questions.

1 How can you keep your heart healthy?

2 Can you explain the meaning of your name?

3 Which lectures do you most enjoy? Why?

4 Do you buy ready-made orange juice or do you squeeze the oranges yourself?

5 Do people in your country often wear hats? Where? Do they remove them inside a building?

6 What do you do to protect your skin in the sun?

B Before you listen

Activating prior knowledge

1 When do you usually drink fruit juices?

I usually drink orange juice …

2 What is the process for making orange juice? Explain it to your partner.

First, …   Then, …   Finally, …

C Global listening

🎧 **6.5** Listen to *Let's concentrate on orange juice*. Answer the questions.

Listening for main ideas

1 What is happening to sales of orange juice?
   a they are going up
   b they are going down
   c they are not changing

2 Which type of orange juice is *not* explained in the lecture?
   a fresh orange juice
   b orange juice from concentrate
   c orange juice not from concentrate

3 Which of the following is *not* a benefit of orange juice?
   a it has vitamin C
   b it has sugar
   c it has vitamin A

4 Why is orange juice less popular these days?
   a people are drinking apple juice instead
   b people prefer coffee
   c it's getting more and more expensive.

D Close listening

The following signals can help you identify the steps in a process:

Key words: *step, process, order, action, do, make*

Sequence words: *first, second, next, after that, finally*

Active voice verbs: *First, scientists take muscle cells from a living cow.*

Passive voice verbs: *Next, the juice is pasteurized.*

Listening for steps in a process

1 🎧 **6.6** Listen to part of the lecture. Choose the signal phrases you hear.

___ after that   ___ next
___ at last   ___ second
___ finally   ___ then
___ first   ___ to begin
___ in the next step   ___ to start

2 🎧 6.7 Listen again to part of the lecture. Use the words in the list to fill in the missing steps in the diagram.

| concentrated | picked | sold | squeezed | transported |

Orange juice production

Step 1: The fruit is
1 _____

Step 2: The juice is
2 _____

Orange juice not from concentrate (nfc)

Orange juice from concentrate (fc)

Step 3: 3 _____

Step 4: 4 _____

Step 5: _reconstituted_

Step 6: _pasteurized_

Step 7: The bottled juice is
5 _____

E Critical thinking

Discuss the questions.

1 Do you prefer to drink juice that is from concentrate or not from concentrate?
   I prefer to drink juice that is concentrated/unconcentrated because…

2 Which type of orange juice from the diagram above is healthier?
   I think … is healthier because…

3 Why is it important to know about how food and drink is made?
   I think it's important to know how food and drink is made because…

Pronunciation for listening

Thought groups and pausing

English speakers usually divide long sentences into shorter groups of words called thought groups. Normally, thought groups are phrases and clauses. Writers use punctuation—commas and periods—to separate these groups. In speaking, there is often a very small pause between thought groups. The pauses give the speaker time to think, and they give the listener time to understand. For example:

You read: *In the next step, most of the water is removed from the juice. In other words, the juice is concentrated. It takes up less space, so it's easier to transport.*

You hear: *In the next step, / most of the water is removed from the juice. / In other words, / the juice is concentrated. / It takes up less space, / so it's easier to transport.*

1 🎧 **6.8** Listen to sentences from *Lab burger*. Notice the pauses. Then listen again and repeat.

  1 OK, / I'll start / by giving you some background information.

  2 As you know / the world's population / is growing very fast.

  3 By the year twenty-fifty / there will be nine billion people / on the planet.

  4 We have to find a way / to feed / all those people.

  5 The process of making meat / in a lab / was first developed by Professor Mark Post / in the Netherlands.

2 🎧 **6.9** Listen to sentences from *Let's concentrate on orange juice*. Write (/) where your hear pauses. Then listen again and repeat.

  1 This lecture is the second in our series on the food industry.

  2 Our topic today is orange juice.

  3 Orange juice is one of the most popular drinks in the world.

  4 In 2010, about three quarters of Americans bought orange juice.

  5 That means 225 million people drank about 7 billion liters every year.

3 Write (/) in the places where you think the speaker will pause.

  1 I'm Marcus, and I'd like to introduce Yasmin.

  2 Scientists take muscle cells from a living cow.

  3 They add egg, breadcrumbs, and some vegetable juice to give it color.

  4 This technology is very new. We can't make large amounts of lab beef yet.

  5 There's orange juice "from concentrate" and orange juice "not from concentrate".

  6 In addition, orange juice also has vitamin A, which helps protect the heart.

Vocabulary development

Sequencers

Sequencers are words that show the sequence or order of steps in a process or story. There are many sequencers for signaling the beginning, middle, and end of a process or story. For example:

Beginning signals: *First, To begin, In the beginning*

Middle signals: *Next, Then, After (that), At the same time, When, While, Second, Third,* etc.

End signals: *Finally, In the end, Last*

🎧 **6.10** Listen again to segments from Listening 1 and Listening 2. Complete each segment with the words in the box.

> First   finally   Next   When

1   The process of making meat in a lab was first developed by Professor Mark Post in the Netherlands, and it has several steps. [1]_____, scientists take muscle cells from a living cow. Don't worry, it doesn't hurt the animal. [2]_____, these cells are allowed to grow and divide in the lab for several weeks until there are billions of them. [3]_____ there are enough cells, the scientists take them and use them to make a hamburger. They add egg, breadcrumbs, and some vegetable juice to give it color and [4]_____ they cook it!

> After that   In the end   Next   To begin

2   [1]_____, I'll explain orange juice from concentrate. In this process, the oranges are first picked from the trees, and the juice is squeezed out of the fruit. In the next step, most of the water is removed from the juice. In other words, the juice is concentrated. It takes up less space, so it's easier to transport. [2]_____, the concentrated juice is transported to factories all over the world. At these factories the juice is reconstituted, which means the water is put back in. [3]_____, the juice is pasteurized. This means it is heated quickly in order to kill any bacteria that can make people sick. [4]_____, the pasteurized juice is put in bottles or cartons and shipped to stores for you to buy.

Academic words

1 Match the words in bold with the correct definition.

1	**percent** (n)	a	a set of similar things that follow each other
2	**technology** (n)	b	to move or carry from one place to another
3	**benefit** (n)	c	someone who works with you
4	**series** (n)	d	advantage
5	**transport** (v)	e	machines, equipment, or devices
6	**colleague** (n)	f	one part of 100

2 Complete the sentences with a word in bold from Exercise 1.

1 We paid $50 for tickets to attend a _____ of ten lectures about food production.

2 Dr. Wasir and her _____, Dr. Sinha, are studying the health benefits of orange juice.

3 It takes weeks to _____ oranges grown in Brazil to juice factories in the United States.

4 In India, almost 30 _____ of people say that they are vegetarian.

5 One _____ of Vitamin A is that it helps people see better at night.

6 Right now, the _____ that is used for making meat in a lab is still very expensive.

3 Work with a partner. Take turns asking and answering the questions. Use the words in parentheses in your answers.

1 A: How many young people in your country attend university?
B: (about / percent).

2 A: Is it hard to build an app?
B: (No / technology / simple).

3 A: Is fish a healthy type of food?
B: (Yes / have / many benefits).

4 A: Are you busy on Thursday nights?
B: (Yes / attend / lecture series / about film making).

5 A: I bought a piano!
B: (Great / how / transport / to your house)?

6 A: Are you giving your presentation by yourself?
B: (No / speak / with / colleague).

Speaking model

You are going to learn about the present passive, explanation signals, and the pronunciation of -ed endings. You will then use these to describe a process diagram.

A Analyze

Read the sentences about how orange juice is made. Write numbers next to the sentences to show the correct order.

1 Today I'll explain the process of making orange juice.   _1_

2 Next, the pasteurized juice is put into bottles.   ___

3 In the third step, the juice is pasteurized.   ___

4 Finally, the juice is sold to customers.   ___

5 First, the oranges are picked.   ___

6 After that, the juice is squeezed from the fruit.   ___

B Discuss

Work with a partner. Answer the questions to help you understand the organization and content of the model.

1 How did you choose the order of the sentences in Exercise A? What helped you?

2 Underline the verbs in the presentation. What tense are they in?

3 Highlight the sequence words. How many are there? Are any of them repeated? Can you think of other words and expressions to replace the sequencers you underlined?

Grammar

Present passive

The present passive is formed by using the verb *be* in the present tense + the past participle of the verb. For example: First, the oranges <u>are picked</u>.

Form: To form a passive sentence, change the object of an active sentence to the subject of a passive one.

<u>Affirmative</u>

Active: (Someone) ships the <u>oranges</u> to factories all over the world.

Passive: <u>Oranges</u> are shipped to factories all over the world.

<u>Negative</u>

Active: They don't pick <u>green oranges</u>.

Passive: <u>Green oranges</u> are not picked.

Use: Use the passive when the "doer" (the subject of the active sentence) is not known or not important. In the active sentence above, we don't know who ships the oranges, and it's not important.

1 Complete the sentences with the passive form of the verb in parentheses.

1 Ralph's supermarket is a busy place at night. The doors (lock) ___*are locked*___ at 11 p.m., and then the work begins.

2 Each night the floor (clean) _____.

3 New items (put) _____ on the shelves.

4 Old fruit, vegetables, bread, and eggs (remove) _____.

5 They (replace) _____ with fresh items.

6 Also, many things (deliver) _____ during the night.

7 The truck (unload) _____ quickly.

8 The items (sell) _____ again the next day.

2 Change the active sentences in parentheses to the passive form.

1 To begin, (a worker attaches a small tag) ___*a small tag is attached*___ to your clothes so that they don't get mixed up with everyone else's.

2 Next, (the workers examine your clothes) _____ for missing buttons, holes, etc.

3 If there are stains on your clothes, (workers clean the clothes) _____ with a special cleaning liquid.

4 Now (the workers load the clothes) _____ into a machine.

5 (The machine cleans your clothes) _____ with a special chemical.

6 (The machine does not use water.) _____.

7 After cleaning, (workers iron your clothes.) _____.

8 Finally, (they fold your clothes). _____.

Speaking skill

Very often, speakers need to explain a word or idea, or they want to give more information about it to make it clearer. The following signals tell your listeners that you are explaining or defining.

I mean …   in other words …   this/that means …   which means …

In the next step, most of the water is removed from the juice. <u>In other words</u>, the juice is concentrated.

1   Complete the items with explanation signals. There may be more than one correct answer. Then compare answers with a partner.

> I mean …   in other words …   this/that means …   which means …

1   In 2010, about three quarters of Americans bought orange juice. _____ 225 million people drank about 7 billion liters every year.

2   Let's talk about orange juice not from concentrate. … There's no concentration step. _____ the water is not removed from the juice.

3   At night, the shelves in a supermarket are restocked, _____ workers put out new food to replace the food that customers bought during the day.

4   The first step in making olive oil is that the olives are picked. _____ they are removed from the tree.

5   In the U.S., the government inspects meat before it is shipped to markets. _____, government workers check the meat to make sure it does not contain bacteria.

6   Los Angeles now has six metro train lines. _____ the public transportation system is getting better and better.

2   Work with a partner. Read the sentences. Then add the explanation signal and define or explain the underlined word or idea. Use a dictionary to help you understand the underlined words and ideas.

1   The U.K. and Saudi Arabia are <u>monarchies</u>. In other words,…

2   It's important to <u>proofread</u> your writing before you give it to your teacher. That means…

3   Some countries <u>don't have enough universities</u>, which means ….

Pronunciation for speaking

-ed endings

The -ed ending, which appears on past-tense verbs and in the passive voice, is pronounced three different ways in English. Here are the rules:

If a verb ends in …	then pronounce the -ed ending as…	Examples
… a voiceless sound (p, k, f, s, sh), voiceless /th/ …	an unvoiced /t/.	picked, shipped
… a voiced sound (b, g, v, z, zh, w, y, all vowels)	a voiced /d/.	allowed, raised, squeezed, removed, worried
/t/ or /d/	a separate syllable, /əd/.	tasted, concentrated, heated

1 **6.11** How is the -ed ending pronounced in the following words? Write the letter A, B, or C next to the words. Then listen to check your answers.

A /t/   B /d/   C /əd/

1 ___ picked
2 ___ transported
3 ___ sliced
4 ___ used

5 ___ separated
6 ___ washed
7 ___ peeled
8 ___ packed

2 Complete the sentences below with words from Exercise 1.

1 A knife is _____ to cut the meat.
2 Olives are _____ in September.
3 White and colored clothes are usually _____ separately.
4 Oranges are _____ by truck.
5 Bananas are _____.
6 Tomatoes are _____ when they are still green.

3 Read the sentences in Exercise 2 with a partner. Focus on your pronunciation of the -ed endings.

Speaking task

Describe a process to a partner. Student A, look at the diagram below. Student B, look at the diagram on page 188.

Brainstorm

Use the diagrams to complete the process. Use the passive form.

How **Olive Oil** is Made

①

The olives (pick) _____ by the farmers in September when the olives are green and ripe.

②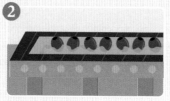

The olives (wash) _____ in cold water to remove the dirt and bacteria.

③

The olives (transport) _____ to a large factory.

④

They (press) _____ by a big machine and the stones (remove) _____. This forms a paste.

⑤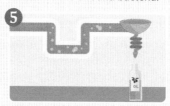

The paste (separate) _____ into oil and water, and the oil goes into a bottle.

⑥

The olive oil (use) _____ with salads and other foods.

Plan

Plan your description of the process. Add the following language from this unit:

- key words for describing a process (page 105)
- passive voice verbs (page 111)
- sequencers (page 108)
- vocabulary from Unit 6

Speak

Practice your description. Focus on the correct pronunciation of -ed endings.

Share

Describe your process to a partner. Point to each picture as you explain the process.

Reflect

Think about the process of making a lab burger, orange juice, olive oil, and potato chips.

Which process …

1 is the most complex?
2 requires the most expensive equipment?
3 takes the most / least time?

Review

Wordlist

MACMILLAN
DICTIONARY

Vocabulary preview

background (n)***	heart (n)***	protect (v)***
beef (n)**	laboratory ("lab") (n)**	remove (v)***
development (n)***	lecture (n)**	squeeze (v)**
disgusting (adj)*	process (n)***	tasty (adj)*
explain (v)***	product (n)***	

Vocabulary development

after (that) (adv)***	first (adv/n)***	second (adv)
at the same time (phrase)	in the beginning (phrase)	then (adj/adv)***
		third (adv)
begin (v)	in the end (phrase)	when (adv)***
finally (adv)***	next (adj/adv)***	while (conj)***

Academic words

benefit (n)***	percent (n)***	technology (n)***
colleague (n)***	series (n)***	transport (v)***

Academic words review

Complete the sentences with the words in the box.

benefit   equipment   expert   instructions   technology

1 When cooking, make sure you follow the _____ and do each step carefully.

2 _____ helps me to be healthy because I use an app to record what I eat and when I exercise.

3 An _____, like a dietician, can tell you what kind of food you should eat.

4 What is one _____ of eating fresh food?

5 Do you need special _____ to make fresh orange juice?

Unit review

Listening 1		I can listen for opinions.
Listening 2		I can listen for steps in a process.
Vocabulary		I can use sequencers.
Grammar		I can use the present passive.
Speaking		I can use explanation signals.
Pronunciation		I can pronounce -ed endings.

7 EXTREMES

Animals VS. Humans

Discussion point

Study the infographic and answer the questions.

1 Which facts from the infographic surprise you the most?

2 Which abilities are humans better at than animals?

3 What is your favorite animal? Why?

GLOSSARY
km/h = kilometers per hour
kms = kilometers
m = meters
kgs = kilograms
mins = minutes

	Animals	Humans
Running speed (on land)	Cheetah 112 km/h	Usain Bolt 45 km/h
Jumping distance	Snow Leopard 15.25 m	Mike Powell 8.95 m
Long distance run	Dog 65 kms	Dean Karnazes 550 kms
Strength (lifting power)	African Elephant 500 kgs	Hossein Rezazadeh 263 kgs
Holding breath underwater	Whale 138 mins	Aleix Segura Vendrell 24:03 mins
Height	Giraffe 5.5 m	Robert Wadlow 2.7 m
Life span	Quahog Clam 507 years	Jeanne Calment 122 years

VIDEO

EXTREME RUNNING

Before you watch

1 You're going to watch a video about an extreme sportsperson. Read the information about a type of sport.

A normal marathon is just over 26 miles or 42 km. An ultramarathon is longer, harder and in difficult places.

2 Discuss the question with a partner.

1 How long, in distance and hours, do you think an ultramarathon is?

2 Where do you think an ultramarathon might take place?

3 What do think the problems might be in running an ultramarathon?

3 Watch the video and check your answers.

UNIT AIMS

LISTENING 1 Understanding categories
LISTENING 2 Listening for words to classify items
STUDY SKILL How do you remember things?

VOCABULARY Regular and extreme adjectives
GRAMMAR Expressing and asking about ability
SPEAKING Giving a short description

A cheetah in Namibia, Africa.

While you watch

Watch the video. Answer the questions.

17   240   2016   direction   partner

1 An ultramarathon can be 160 or _____ km long.

2 Simon lost his sight when he was _____.

3 When Simon runs in the city he has a running _____.

4 The app was created to help Simon run in the right _____.

5 Simon entered the Namibian ultramarathon in May _____.

After you watch

Work with a partner. Discuss the questions.

1 What do you think about Simon and the ultramarathon?

   I think Simon was … (adjective) because …

2 Would you like to take part in an extreme sport?

   I personally would / would not do extreme sports, such as … because …

3 What other ways can technology help blind or disabled athletes?

   Technology like apps can help because …

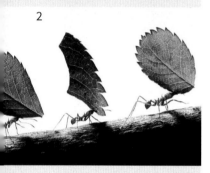

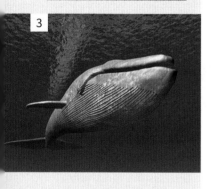

LISTENING

Amazing creatures

A Vocabulary preview

1   Read these sentences. Match the words in bold with the correct definition.

   1   The giraffe is an **amazing** animal. Did you know they sleep standing up?

   2   The **average** weight of an elephant's brain is just over 5 kg.

   3   There are many different **categories** of animal, for example mammals, birds, and fish.

   4   I think the most interesting **fact** about the snow leopard is that it can jump over 15 meters.

   5   The heaviest animal on the planet is the blue whale. They **weigh** about 190,000 kg.

   6   A mosquito is a type of **insect** which, in Spanish, means "little fly".

   a   _____ (n) a piece of true information

   b   _____ (v) to describe how heavy something is

   c   _____ (n) a small creature with six legs, like a bee or a fly

   d   _____ (n) groups that have similar characteristics

   e   _____ (adj) extremely good

   f   _____ (adj) around typical amount, level, or standard

2   Look at the sentences again in Exercise 1. Which one is the most interesting fact? Discuss with a partner.

B Before you listen

1   Match the picture with the correct animal. Use a dictionary to help you. What do you know about each animal?

   Ant   Lyrebird   Sailfish   Blue Whale

2   Complete each column of the table with the two words from the box. Use a dictionary to help you.

   ~~call~~   enormous   quick   repeat   slow-moving   strong   tiny   weak

Communication	Size	Speed	Strength
call			

C Global listening

1 🎧 **7.1** Listen to the first part of *Amazing creatures* and choose the correct answer to complete each sentence.

Listening for main ideas

1 The speakers are talking about a …
   a book they have read.
   b lesson for an elementary class.
   c documentary movie.

2 Jennah has a problem with …
   a thinking of a topic.
   b finding interesting facts.
   c organizing the information.

3 Miwa suggests that Jennah should arrange the information by …
   a types of features or abilities.
   b types of environment.
   c types of animals.

4 Jennah thinks that Miwa's idea is …
   a not interesting.
   b good.
   c interesting but not possible.

When listening to a talk or lecture, it's a good idea to try and put the information into categories. This will help you to understand the structure of the talk and the different types of information the speaker is giving. For example, when listening to the lecture about amazing creatures, listen for words that fit into these categories:

Category	Common words
Communication	*talk, speak*
Size	*big, small*
Speed	*fast, slow*
Strength	*power, strong*

Understanding categories

2 🎧 **7.2** Listen to the second part of *Amazing creatures*. Match the animal with the correct category.

1	Lyrebird	a	Size
2	Sailfish	b	Communication
3	Ant	c	Strength
4	Blue Whale	d	Speed

Taking notes while listening

D Close listening

1 🎧 **7.2** Listen again to the second part of *Amazing creatures*. Complete each note with one word or number.

Animal	Notes
Lyrebird	*Can produce sounds of* [1]_____ *different bird species*
Sailfish	*Can* [2]_____ *110 kms per hour*
Ant	*Can lift and carry* [3]_____ *times its body weight*
Blue Whale	*Brain weighs nearly* [4]_____ *kgs*

2 🎧 **7.2** Listen again and make notes of two more interesting facts you learned from *Amazing creatures*. Then compare with a partner.

1 _____.

2 _____.

E Critical thinking

Discuss the questions.

1 Which do you think is the most impressive animal from *Amazing creatures*? Why?

I think the most impressive animal is the …

2 Which animals would you include in a project about amazing creatures?

I would include … because …

3 How would you organize a project about amazing creatures?

I would organize it by … because …

Pronunciation for listening

Glottal stop

When a word ends with /t/ and the following word begins with a consonant, the final /t/ in the first word is not fully pronounced. Instead, the voice is stopped very quickly before saying the next word. This is also known as a glottal stop.

1 🎤 **7.3** Look at the sentences below. Underline the places where final /t/ comes before another consonant. Then listen and notice the pronunciation.

1 Can you think of different categories?
2 Tell me about some amazing animal facts.
3 Most people think that the cheetah is the fastest animal.
4 I think that could work.
5 That makes sense.
6 The strongest creature is tiny.

2 🎤 **7.4** Listen to the sentences below and write in the missing words. Then listen again and notice the pronunciation.

1 I'm _____ sure how to organize my information.
2 How long can _____ people hold their breath?
3 Here's one _____ lyrebirds.
4 _____ falls into the category of communication.
5 Which animal has the _____ brain?
6 The _____ category is size.
7 Ok, how about strength? _____ me guess… elephants, right?
8 That's equal to a bodybuilder being able to _____ 3,700 kgs.

3 With a partner, take turns saying the sentences from Exercise 2. Notice how the final /t/ is pronounced when it comes before a word beginning with a consonant.

Ultimate memory

A Vocabulary preview

1 Match the words in bold with the correct definition.

1	**technique** (n)	a	a piece of writing in which the words are arranged on separate lines
2	**remember** (v)	b	occasions or activities that happen or are planned
3	**poem** (n)	c	not to forget
4	**events** (n)	d	a specific way of doing a task or exercise
5	**cases** (n)	e	where information or ideas have come from, e.g. a report, an expert, a set of rules
6	**calendar** (n)	f	something you remember, like information, experiences, or dates
7	**according to** (prep)	g	specific situations
8	**memory** (n)	h	a printed table showing all the days, weeks, and months of the year

2 Complete each sentence with a word in bold from Exercise 1.

1 I can remember special _____ clearly, like my first day at school.

2 I know a very effective _____ for remembering information for a test.

3 If I read a _____ that I really like, I can usually remember every line of it.

4 I can _____ the first day I went to school.

5 I always write down important dates on a _____.

6 I know many _____ of weak students who get good grades because they study hard.

7 I don't have a very good _____ and I often forget important dates, like birthdays.

8 _____ my teacher, my English is getting much better.

3 Work with a partner. Which sentences are true for you?

B Before you listen

Activating prior knowledge

1 Discuss the questions with a partner.

1 Do you have a good memory?   *I have a very good/bad memory …*

2 What things do you remember best?   *I am good at remembering …*

3 What things do you often forget?   *I often forget …*

2 Complete the memory test with a partner.

1 Look at the picture for 30 seconds. Close your books. With a partner, write down everything you can remember in the picture.

2 Look at the number for 30 seconds. Close your books. With a partner, write down the number in the exact order.

1234998778055528041183

C Global listening

1 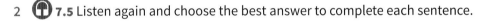 **7.5** Listen to *Ultimate memory* and number the topics in order.

Listening for main ideas

___ Types of extreme memory

___ People with "super memorization"

_1_ Dr. Alvi's book

___ A sentence to help remember facts

___ People with "event memory"

2 **7.5** Listen again and choose the best answer to complete each sentence.

1 Dr. Alvi talks about his new…

   a movie.   b book.   c chat show.

2 According to Dr. Alvi, there are … categories of memory.

   a two   b three   c four

3 Brad Williams and Jill Price are examples of…

   a event memorizers.

   b super memorizers.

   c both event and super memorizers.

4 Tatiana Cooley and Wang Feng are examples of…

   a event memorizers.

   b super memorizers.

   c both event and super memorizers.

5 The sentence, "My very energetic mother just served us noodles" can help you …

   a learn English grammar.

   b discuss meal-time customs.

   c memorize the order of the planets.

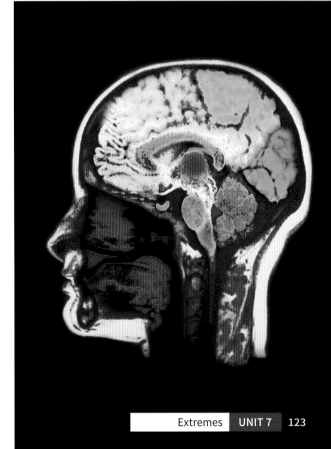

Listening for words
used to classify items

D Close listening

> In presentations, lectures, and news reports, speakers often organize items according to features or qualities they have in common. Listening for the words speakers use to classify people, things, and ideas helps you to understand and organize the information. For example:
>
> verbs: *categorize, classify, divide, fall into, fit into, put into*
>
> nouns: *category, class, group, kind (of), type (of)*

1 🎧 7.6 Listen to excerpts from *Ultimate memory*. Complete these sentences. Then write *V* (verb) or *N* (noun) next to each expression.

1 That means we _____ into that very large _____ of people called … normal!

2 Now, psychologists usually _____ them into two _____.

3 We can _____ them into different _____, like using an image, a story, or a sentence.

2 🎧 7.7 Listen and complete these sentences about classifying information. Then underline the information that is being classified.

1 At this university the course subjects _____ four _____: physical sciences, social sciences, humanities, and technology.

2 The food we eat is usually _____ four _____: dairy products, fruits and vegetables, grains, and meat.

3 Psychologists often _____ people into two _____: A personality and B personality.

4 My teacher often says that students _____ two _____: hardworking or lazy.

5 Libraries use many different systems to _____ books into several _____.

E Critical thinking

Discuss the questions.

1 Which example of extreme memory impresses you the most? Why?

I'm most impressed by … because …

2 Would you like to have extreme event memory? Why or why not? Think about exams, on vacations, at work, or with your hobbies.

I would/wouldn't like to have an extreme event memory because …

3 Do you think it is possible to train your memory to become better?

I think it's possible/impossible to train your memory …

Study skills — How do you remember things?

1 When is your best friend's birthday?
2 Who were your elementary school teachers?
3 What was your first day at school like?
4 What did you wear yesterday?
5 How do you get to the nearest post office?

© Stella Cottrell (2013)

1 How do you remember things? Try to recall each of the items 1–5 above. After each one, note down what you did to help you remember.

2 Answer the questions below. Then compare your answers with a partner.

1 How many of the items in Exercise 1 could you recall?
2 Which item was the easiest to recall? Why?
3 Which item was the most difficult to recall? Why?
4 Did you use any special ways to help you remember the items? What are they?

3 Do you have any memories of experiences when you felt an extreme emotion: happy, sad, angry, surprised, disappointed, afraid, or nervous? Make notes in the chart below.

How old were you?	Where?	Who with?	What happened?	How did you feel?

4 Use your notes to tell a partner about one of your experiences.

I remember when I was … years old …
I was at / in …
was with …
I felt very …

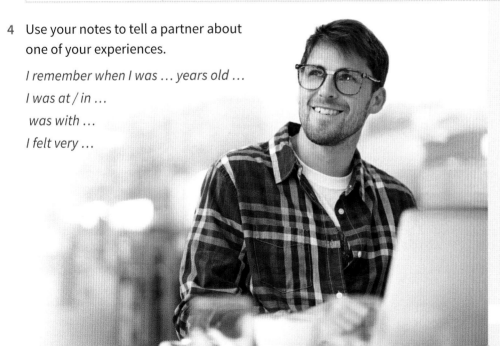

Vocabulary development

-ed and -ing adjectives

Some adjectives can take an -ed ending and an -ing ending. For example:

Adjectives with -ed ending: *amazed, annoyed, bored, fascinated, frightened, interested, tired*

Adjectives with -ing ending: *amazing, annoying, boring, fascinating, frightening, interesting, tiring*

Adjectives that end in -ed are used to describe how someone feels.

I'm excited about my new English course.
She felt tired after her day of lectures.

Adjectives that end in -ing are used to describe the characteristics of a person, thing, or situation.

My mechanical engineering class is really interesting.
The cheetah is a fascinating animal.

We usually use the pronouns *I, you, he, she, we,* and *they* with -ed adjectives. We usually use the pronoun *it* with -ing adjectives. We can also use verbs like *look, seem,* and *sound* with both -ed and -ing adjectives.

A: *I'm going to a lecture tomorrow evening all about the lyrebird.*
B: *Great! It sounds very interesting.*

A: *I'm worried about Sarah. I think she's working too hard.*
B: *You're right. She looks really tired.*

1 Complete the sentences below with the correct form of the adjective in bold.

1 You look really **tired / tiring**. You should go to bed.

2 I'm really **interested / interesting** in cars.

3 My professor always gives us too much homework. It's so **annoyed / annoying**.

4 A turtle can live for up to 150 years. It's an **amazed /amazing** animal!

5 I am going to see a lecture on super memory next week. I'm really **excited / exciting**.

6 I find science a really **bored / boring** subject. That's why I study modern languages.

2 Describe an animal that you know well to a partner. Use the adjectives from the skills box, Exercise 1, and the information on page 120 to help you. Your partner must guess the animal.

This animal is really interesting, it is/has …
I am really frightened of this animal, it is/has …

Academic words

1 Read the sentences. Match the words in bold with the correct definition.

   1 Many people believe that Finland has the best education **system** in the world.

   2 I have read about an **individual** in China who has ultimate memory.

   3 People learn to speak English in many different ways. There is no one best **method**.

   4 After I read an article, I usually remember the main ideas, but not all the **details**.

   5 Make sure all of the facts in your essay are **accurate** before handing it in to the teacher.

   a _____ (n)   the particular facts or pieces of information about a topic or idea

   b _____ (n)   a group or set of parts that work together to achieve a purpose

   c _____ (adj) correct and without any errors or mistakes

   d _____ (n)   relating to one person and not a group

   e _____ (n)   a careful and organized plan for doing something

2 Answer the questions and explain your answers to a partner.

   1 Is it easy for you to remember the details of stories and articles you read?

   2 Is the grammatical system of English easier or more difficult than in your native language?

   3 Do you think there is one best method for learning English?

   4 Do you know any individuals who can memorize information very easily?

   5 Is all of the information on your social media profile accurate?

Speaking model

You are going to learn about expressing and asking about ability, pronouncing *can* and *can't*, and language for giving a description. You are then going to use these to complete a memory questionnaire and then give a description about ability.

A Analyze

1 Work with a partner. Complete the model with the correct word from the box.

> copy   find   perfectly   reasons   special   strong

> Today, I would like to talk about the lyrebird. The lyrebird is a small bird with ¹_____ legs and feet and you can ²_____ them mainly in the forests and national parks of Australia. The female lyrebird is about 80 cm long and the male is slightly longer, about 90 cm long. The lyrebird has a very ³_____ skill. It is able to ⁴_____ sounds from the environment, including car alarms, cameras, and crying babies. Zoologists believe that they can produce 20 different species of bird song ⁵_____. They are also very beautiful animals and they often display their feathers. For these ⁶_____, the lyrebird is one of my favorite types of animal.

2 Underline the phrase that introduces the description.

3 What phrase does the speaker use to describe the size of the female lyrebird?

4 Underline all the instances of *can* and *be able to*. What type of word follows *can* and *be able to*?

5 What phrase does the speaker use to end the description?

B Discuss

1 What bird or animals are considered to be special in your country? Why?
   In my country, the … is considered …

2 Do you have a favorite type of bird or animal? If yes, which one? Why?
   My favorite type of … is …

Grammar

Expressing and asking about ability

We can express and ask about ability using *can* and *be able to*. Study the forms:

Form	Example
<u>Present ability</u>	
subject + *can* + base form	*It can swim 100 meters in 4.8 seconds.*
subject + *cannot/can't* + base form	*I can't remember what I did yesterday.*
subject + *is/are* + able to + base form	*He's able to memorize the exact order of 52 cards*
subject + *is not / are not* + able to + base form	*I'm not able to run 10 kilometers.*
<u>Wh- questions</u>	
Wh- + *can* + subject + base form	*What can you remember from the story?*
Wh- + *is/are* + subject + *able to* + base form	*What are you able to recall about that day?*
<u>Yes/no questions</u>	
Can + subject + base form	*Can you remember the teachers' names?* (*Yes, I can. / No, I cannot/can't.*)
Is/Are + subject + *able to* + base form	*Are you able to remember the details?* (*Yes, I am. / No, I am not.*)

1   Find the mistake in each sentence.

   1   I can to speak German.
   2   They are to able swim very fast.
   3   Miki is can recall all the details of the movie.
   4   That animal is able survive without water.
   5   He cans memorize a long poem perfectly.
   6   I am able for recall all major news events.

2   Change the statements from Exercise 1 into the negative.

3   Rearrange the words below to form questions.

   1   able / are / you / memorize / phone numbers / to ?
   2   languages / you / what / speak / can ?
   3   remember / what / childhood / you / can / about / your ?
   4   recall / you / can / did / weekend / last / you / what ?
   5   sing / many / can / how / English / you / songs / in ?

4   Ask and answer the questions in Exercise 3 with a partner.

Speaking skill

When giving a description, it's important to organize your ideas so that your audience can follow what you are saying. It also helps you to speak more fluently. One method is to divide your talk into sections or categories.

1   Give a short introduction

I am going to talk about the dusky dolphin.

2   Describe the size

The dusky dolphins in New Zealand are about 170 cm long.

3   Describe the appearance

The dusky dolphin has a long, gray tail.

4   Describe the ability

The dusky dolphin can perform different types of jumps.

5   Ending the description

For these reasons, the dusky dolphin is my favorite type of animal.

1   Look at the description of the lyrebird on page 128. Complete the information with phrases from the description.

   1   phrase to give a short introduction

      _____

   2   phrase that describes the size of the lyrebird

      _____

   3   phrase that describes the ability of the lyrebird

      _____

   4   phrase that describes the appearance of the lyrebird

      _____

   5   phrase to end the description

      _____

2   Write a sentence about each animal using phrases from the Skill box or Exercise 1.

Female lyrebird – about 80cm – long   *The female lyrebird is about 80cm long.*

Describe the size   Describe the ability

Giraffe – 5.5m – tall   Elephant – lift – 500 kgs

1   _____   3   _____

Describe the appearance   Describe the ability

Arabian camel – a long neck   Falcon – dive – 390 km/h

2   _____   4   _____

Pronunciation for speaking

Pronouncing can/can't; be able to / not able to

Can / Can't

In spoken English *can* is usually used in its reduced or weak form. In this case, it is unstressed and the following verb is stressed.

can **go**   can **remember**   can **sing**

Can't is stressed and it is spoken in its strong form.

can't go   **can't remember**   **can't sing**

We say *can* in its strong, stressed form when we are giving a short answer to a question about ability or possibility.

Can you **play football**?   **yes, i can**.

Be able to / not able to

In spoken English *be able to* is usually used with *be* in its weak contracted form. In this case, *able* receives more stress:

I'm **able** to   *She's* **able** to   *You're* **able** to

not able to is spoken with the stress on **not**:

She's **not** able to pass this course.

1 🎧 7.8 Listen and complete these sentences with *can* or *can't*. Then listen again and repeat.

   1 Brad _____ remember what happened 20 years ago.
   2 Jill _____ remember what time her class begins.
   3 Many people _____ speak more than one language.
   4 Sarah _____ memorize a long poem in ten minutes.
   5 _____ humans live in very extreme environments?
   6 Maria _____ understand the homework assignment.

2 Work with a partner. Take turns asking these questions, and giving short answers. Focus on your pronunciation of *can / can't* and *be able to / not able to*.

   1 Can you swim?
   2 Can you memorize the order of a pack of playing cards?
   3 Can you cook?
   4 Can you run five kilometers?
   5 Are you able to understand a news report in English?
   6 Are you able to give a speech in English?

Speaking task

Complete a memory questionnaire and then give a presentation about an animal.

Memory questionnaire

What information can you remember about each animal from *Amazing creatures*? Give one fact about each animal.

> Lyrebird   Sailfish   Blue Whale   Ant

Brainstorm

Choose one animal you know well. Write five facts about the animal. Think about size, ability and appearance.

1	
2	
3	
4	
5	

Plan

Look at the information in your brainstorm. Prepare a presentation. Use the phrases from page 130 and include the following points.

- A short introduction
- Size
- Ability
- Appearance
- Ending the description

Speak

Work with a partner. Give your presentation. Remember your pronunciation for expressions of ability on page 131. Make notes on your partner's description.

Share

Form a group. Use your notes to describe your partner's animal.

Reflect

Look back at what you have learnt in this unit. Answer the questions.

1 What animal ability on page 116 do you like the most/least? Why?
2 What memory skill on page 124 is the most/least interesting to you? Why?
3 Do you have a good memory? How can you improve it?

Review

Wordlist

MACMILLAN DICTIONARY

Vocabulary preview

according to (v)***	categories (n)	species (n)***
amazing (adj)**	event (n)***	technique (n)***
average (n)***	fact (n)***	weigh (v)**
cases (n)***	poem (n)***	

Vocabulary development

bad (adj)***	fascinating (adj)**	
beautiful (adj)***	freezing (adj)*	interesting (adj)***
big (adj)***	good (adj)***	small (adj)***
boiling (adj)*	gorgeous (adj)*	terrible (adj)***
cold (adj)***	hot (adj)***	tiny (adj)***
fantastic (adj)**	huge (adj)***	

Academic words

accurate (adj)**	individual (adj)***	system (n)***
details (n)***	method (n)***	

Academic words review

Complete the sentences with the words in the box.

area   contact   details   percent   system

1 Please fill in the form with your contact _____.
2 Bamboo makes up about ninety-nine _____ of a giant panda's diet.
3 The bumble bee bat is found in an _____ of Thailand.
4 There is a problem with the computer _____. I can't send e-mails.
5 I usually _____ my friends via social media.

Unit review

Listening 1	I can understand categories.
Listening 2	I can listen for words to classify items.
Vocabulary	I can use regular and extreme adjectives.
Grammar	I can express and ask about ability.
Speaking	I can give a short description.
Pronunciation	I can pronounce *can, can't, be able to / not able to*.

8 VISION

EYE  FACTS

Discussion point

Study the infographic and answer the questions.

1 What day is World Sight Day?
2 How many people in the world are blind?
3 How old are most blind people?

1 October 9th is World Sight Day.

2 Every **5 seconds** someone in the world goes blind.

3 **39 million** people worldwide are blind and **246 million** are visually impaired.

4 With today's technology, we can prevent or treat **80%** of blindness in the world.

5 **82%** of people with blindness are over the age of 50.

6 About **90%** of the world's visually impaired people live in poor areas.

7 Since 1991, more than **40 million** people worldwide have had LASIK – a surgery to correct poor vision.

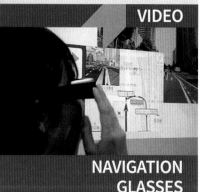

VIDEO

NAVIGATION GLASSES

Before you watch

Discuss the questions with a partner. Use a dictionary to help you understand the words in bold.

1 Are you good at **navigating** around a new place when you go on holiday?
2 When you are a tourist, do you prefer to use a traditional map or your smartphone to give you **directions**?
3 Can you remember a time when you, or someone you know, got lost in a building or city? How did you **find your way**?

UNIT AIMS

LISTENING 1 Recognizing numbers
LISTENING 2 Identifying descriptive details
STUDY SKILL Rounding up and down

VOCABULARY Words for talking about a photograph
GRAMMAR Gerunds and infinitives
SPEAKING Phrases to describe location

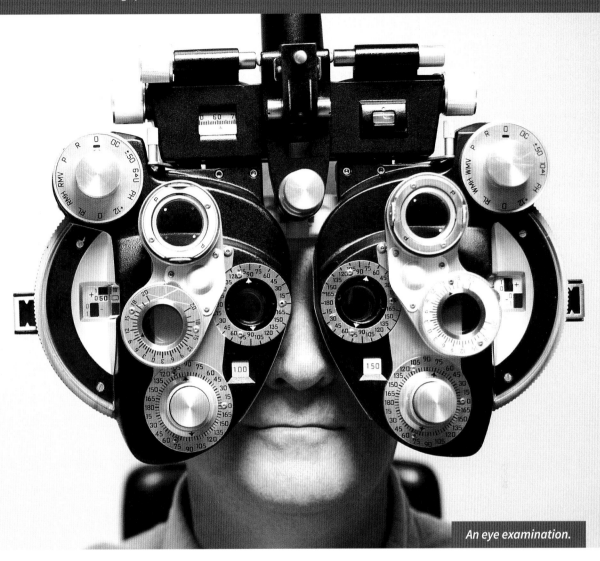

An eye examination.

While you watch

Watch the video and choose *T* (True) or *F* (False).

1 The IT exhibition is in China.   T / F

2 The glasses are a new invention.   T / F

3 The glasses are connected to a cell phone.   T / F

4 The woman says she would not like to use the product.   T / F

5 The main reason for the exhibition is to attract tourists.   T / F

After you watch

Work with a partner. Discuss the questions.

1 In which cities would it be good to have navigation glasses?
I think it would be a good idea to have them in …

2 Are the navigation glasses a good invention? Why? / Why not?
I think they are a good invention because …
One problem with the glasses is that …

3 Is this new technology, or is it similar to something that you already have?
It is new technology because the engineer in the video says …
I think it is similar to …

How we see the world

A Vocabulary preview

1 Match the words in bold with the correct definition.

1 I **blink** approximately 20 times per minute.
2 Sometimes I don't **notice** when my friend is speaking.
3 In my country, **blind** people use a white cane when they are in public.
4 I like wearing clothes in all colors **except** brown.
5 I don't have good **vision** at night, so I don't like to drive when it's dark.
6 When sitting, it's important that your back and legs form an angle of 90 **degrees**.
7 My **sense** of sight is not very strong. I need to wear glasses.
8 When I take a test, I always check my answers **twice.**

a _____ (prep) not including
b _____ (v) to open and close your eyes quickly
c _____ (adj) not able to see
d _____ (v) to see or become aware of something
e _____ (adv) two times
f _____ (n) natural physical abilities: to see, hear, smell, taste, or feel
g _____ (n) the ability to see
h _____ (n) a way of measuring angles, written with the symbol °

2 Work with a partner. Which of the sentences in Exercise 1 are true for you?

B Before you listen

Activating prior knowledge

1 Look at the pictures on page 137. Discuss the questions with a partner. Which animal do you think …

1 sees the best from far away?
2 sees the best at night?
3 uses sound to locate food?

I think … sees the best from far away.

2 What do you think the following phrases mean? Do you have similar expressions in your language?

blind as a bat   eagle-eyed

I think "blind as a bat" means …   In my language we say …

C Global listening

1 🎧 **8.1** Listen to an interview about vision. Put the topics in the order that the speakers discuss them. One topic is not discussed.

___ vision in bats

_1_ how many parts of the eye

___ seeing in color

___ distance humans can see

___ vision in birds

___ blinking

2 Look back at the questions in Part B on page 136. Were your guesses correct?

Listening for main ideas

Eagle

Bat

Owl

D Close listening

Recognizing numbers

> Numbers can be difficult to understand, especially when a speaker talks quickly. Listen for these words to help you recognize a number: *hundred, thousand, hundred thousand, million, percent,* and *point.*
>
> | | |
> |---|---|
> | 215 | two hundred and fifteen |
> | 2,750 | two thousand seven hundred and fifty |
> | 27,551 | twenty-seven thousand five hundred and fifty-one |
> | 275,552 | two hundred seventy-five thousand five hundred and fifty-two |
> | 2,750,000 | two million seven hundred fifty thousand |
> | 30% | thirty percent |
> | 4.5 | four point five |

1 🎧 8.1 Listen to the interview again. Match the numbers with the notes.

1	2 million	a	% of eye exposed to outside world
2	17	b	working parts in human eye
3	10,000	c	kms humans see on flat land
4	4.6	d	degrees an owl can turn its head
5	100	e	mtrs an owl can see a mouse at night
6	270	f	average # of times we blink in a day

2 🎧 8.2 Listen and choose the correct option to complete the facts.

1 People read **1.5 / 2.5** times slower on a computer screen.

2 My eyeglasses are not so expensive. They cost $ **250 / 260**.

3 This survey shows that **35 / 39** % of teenagers wear glasses.

4 Honey bees have **5,000 / 5,500** lenses in each eye.

5 Falcons can see **2.6 / 6.2** times better than humans.

6 We can see the moon, which is **383,313 / 384,403** kms. away.

E Critical thinking

Discuss the questions.

1 Look again at Exercise 1 and Exercise 2. Which facts surprise you the most?

2 In the future, do you think technology will help people to see better? How?

3 Do you think sight is the most important sense? Why / Why not?

Study skills Rounding up and down

You might know about *rounding up* or *rounding down* when you use money. For example, if you need to pay 4 dollars and 75 cents, you can round up and pay 5 dollars. Or, if you need to pay 4 dollars and 10 cents, you can round down to just 4 dollars.

To speak about rounded numbers, you can use words like *about*, *approximately*, or *more or less*. You can say:

I paid about 5 dollars.   *It costs approximately 5 dollars.*
It costs more or less 5 dollars.

Rounding numbers is similar to rounding money. You can round up or down. For example:

Exact number		Rounded number
986.748	round down to	986.7
986.98	round up to	987
986.752	round up to	986.8 or 987

1 Work with a partner. Round the numbers up or down to one decimal place. Practice saying the rounded number.

It's 41 point 3.

1	41.36	5	1.714
2	912.17	6	10.08
3	22.222	7	66.55
4	99.88	8	6.10987

© Stella Cottrell (2013)

2 🎧 8.3 Listen and choose the numbers you hear.

1 30.8 / 38.8   5 7,779 / 779
2 1.4 / 1.14   6 18,891.26 / 18,809.26
3 11.6 / 1.06   7 190,998 / 190,000.98
4 660.72 / 660,072   8 2,045,049 / 245,849

3 Look at the numbers you chose in Exercise 2. Round the numbers up or down. There can be more than one correct answer.

1	_____	5	_____
2	_____	6	_____
3	_____	7	_____
4	_____	8	_____

A great photograph

A Vocabulary preview

1 Match the words in bold with the correct definitions.

1	**photograph** (n)	a	the flat glass on a computer or phone
2	**screen** (n)	b	a distance of something from top to bottom, e.g. the ocean
3	**square** (n)		
4	**depth** (n)	c	a picture or something you make with a camera
5	**background** (n)	d	a shape with four equal sides and four equal corners
6	**landscape** (n)	e	to take a photograph or picture of something
7	**shoot** (v)	f	the way someone's body or an object is placed
8	**position** (n)	g	an area of land
		h	the back part of a picture or photograph (opposite: foreground)

2 Complete the sentences with the words in bold from Exercise 1.

1 I have two computer _____ at home to play games on.

2 I can swim down to a _____ of five meters.

3 I really like to share _____ of my friends and family on social media.

4 The windows in my bedroom have a _____ shape.

5 I really like _____ photographs, with mountains, trees, and lakes.

6 In group photographs I prefer to stand in the _____ because I'm shy.

7 I am terrible at taking selfies. I can never get into the right _____.

8 I can _____ great pictures using the camera on my cell phone.

3 Work with a partner. Which sentences in Exercise 2 are true for you?

B Before you listen

Activating prior knowledge

Discuss the questions with a partner.

1 Do you enjoy taking photographs?

2 Look at the three photographs below. Are these good photographs? Why or why not?

3 Which photograph is your favorite? Why?

a    b    c

C Global listening

1 🎧 **8.4** Listen to the first part of *A great photograph*. Fill in the missing words.

LISTENING 2

Listening for main ideas

Tips for taking great photographs

📷 **1** Keep it ¹_____

📷 **2** Don't put your main subject in the exact ²_____ of the photographs

📷 **3** Give your photos some ³_____

📷 **4** Shoot from a ⁴_____ angle

2 🎧 **8.5** Listen to the second part of the podcast. Choose the correct answer to complete the sentence.

1 The main subject is the speaker's **brother / sister**.

2 The background is divided into **3 / 4** horizontal parts.

3 The speaker likes the photograph because it's a **beautiful / peaceful** scene.

GLOSSARY

feature (n) an important part of something like a camera or computer

grid (n) a pattern of straight lines that cross each other to make squares

horizontal (adj) parallel to the ground

shot (n) a photograph

vertical (adj) standing straight up

D Close listening

1 🎧 **8.4** Listen and choose *T* (True) or *F* (False) for each sentence.

1 A good photograph should have more than three main subjects.   T / F
2 You can find the grid feature on your phone camera in Settings.   T / F
3 Place your subject at the place where the vertical and horizontal lines meet.   T / F
4 To give your photographs depth, place your subjects in the foreground only.   T / F
5 Your photographs can be more interesting if you shoot while you're lying down.   T / F

Identifying descriptive details

> Descriptive details tell a listener what something looks like. To identify descriptive details, listen for information about a subject's size, color, shape, character, or location. For example:
>
> Size: *big, enormous, small, tiny*
> Color: *red, blue, dark, light, bright*
> Shape: *square, round, long, short*
> Character: *quiet, funny, sad, unusual*
> Location: *in the background, under, next to*

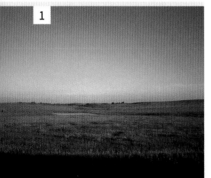

2 🎧 **8.5** Listen again to the second part of the podcast. Choose the correct word to complete the sentences.

1 The photograph was taken in the **morning / afternoon**.
2 The water looks calm and **cold / warm**.
3 The background is divided into three **horizontal / vertical** parts.
4 The trees are in the middle and the mountain is in the **foreground / background**.
5 The photographer took the photograph from a **low / high** angle, which makes the mountain look **smaller / taller**.

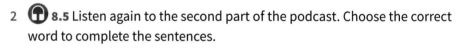

E Critical thinking

Discuss the questions.

1 Look at the three photographs. What is the problem with each one? How could you improve each photograph?
2 What makes the best smartphone photograph? Think about the tips above.
3 Do you think photography is an interesting career? Why / Why not?

Pronunciation for listening

Stress in numbers

Stress can help you to tell the difference between numbers that end in -*teen* and -*ty*. The following rules will help you to decide which number a speaker is saying.

- The last syllable is usually stressed with numbers ending in -*teen*
  fif**teen**, six**teen**, seven**teen**
- The /t/ sound in -*teen* is pronounced as /t/ and not /d/.
  /fɪfˈtiːn/, /sɪkˈstiːn/, /sevənˈtiːn/
- The first syllable is always stressed in numbers ending in -*ty*
  fifty, **six**ty, **se**venty
- The /t/ sound in -*ty* can sometimes sound like a /d/ sound.
  /ˈfɪfdi/, /ˈsɪksdi/, /ˈsevəndɪ/

1 🎧 8.6 Read the numbers below. Then listen and repeat.

1	thirteen	thirty
2	fourteen	forty
3	fifteen	fifty
4	sixteen	sixty
5	seventeen	seventy
6	eighteen	eighty
7	nineteen	ninety

2 🎧 8.7 Listen to excerpts below. Complete each sentence with the correct number.

1 That means our eyes can focus on _____ things per second.

2 Only _____% of our eye is exposed to the outside world.

3 They allow us to blink, on average, _____ times every minute that we're awake.

4 I started taking photographs when I was _____ years old.

5 The average lifespan of an Indiana bat is about _____ years.

6 There are over _____ different species of eagle.

Vocabulary development

Words for talking about a photograph

1   Match the words in bold with the correct definition.

1	**picture** (n)	a	the view in a picture or photo
2	**photographer** (n)	b	how big or small something is
3	**scene** (n)	c	a person who takes pictures
4	**size** (n)	d	a painting, drawing, or photograph
5	**mood** (n)	e	a border around a picture or photo
6	**frame** (n)	f	an area of darkness, created when something blocks the light
7	**shadow** (n)		
8	**contrast** (n)	g	a difference, for example between light and dark
		h	the general feeling in a photo, such as happy or sad.

2   Use the words in bold from Exercise 1 to complete the descriptions of the photos.

Photo A

1   This is a _____ of a young family.

2   It is a _____ of a family in a park.

3   The _____ of the photo is happy because everyone is smiling.

Photo B

4   This is a black and white photo taken by the famous _____ Ansel Adams in 1927. It is in the National Gallery of Art in Washington, D.C.

5   The _____ of the original photo is small: Only 15 X 20 cm.

6   On the upper left side we can see the _____ of a cloud against the mountain.

7   There is a black _____ around the photo.

8   There is a very strong _____ between the light snow and the dark mountains.

3   Use the camera on your cell phone to take two photos: a portrait and a landscape. Work with a partner. Use the words in Exercise 1 to make sentences about your photos.

Academic words

1 Read the sentences. Match the word in bold with the correct definition.

1 A fish similar to a shrimp has the most **complex** vision of any animal in the world.

2 In 2015, the most popular **location** for photographs was the Eiffel Tower in Paris.

3 **Adults** in many cultures prefer the color blue, but children prefer red.

4 It is impossible to take **professional** photographs with a cell phone.

5 On a smartphone, you can change the **focus** of an image by tapping on it.

6 The first photograph was taken in 1826 by a photographer **called** Joseph Niépce.

a _____ (n) the place where something happens

b _____ (n) how clear or unclear a subject in a photo is

c _____ (adj) giving a person or things a name.

d _____ (n) people who are no longer children or teenagers

e _____ (adj) complicated; having many details or small parts

f _____ (adj) having the highest level of skill or quality

2 Work with a partner. Are the sentences in Exercise 1 true or false? If you think a sentence is false, try to correct it.

3 Discuss the questions with a partner.

1 Would you like to be a professional photographer in the future? Why or why not?

2 Do adults take better photographs than children?

3 Do you know how to change the focus on your camera, or do you always use auto-focus?

4 What is a nice location for taking photos at a wedding?

5 Have you ever used a film camera? Was it complex to use?

6 Do you know what the different parts of a camera are called?

Speaking model

You are going to learn about gerunds and infinitives, describing a photo, and pronouncing /p/ and /b/. You are then going to use these to describe a photograph.

A Analyze

Here is a photograph I took two years ago. It shows my friends Marcus and Robert on a camping vacation in Oregon, U.S.A. Marcus is the one in the middle with the blue jacket. Robert is the one next to our blue tent. In the background, you can see Mount Jefferson, which is the second highest mountain in Oregon. There is a shadow because it was early in the morning. In the foreground, you can see some red wildflowers. You can see that my friends are looking at something. Believe it or not, they're looking at a group of wild horses! I really like this photograph because the light and focus are excellent, and the scene is beautiful. Marcus, Robert, and I try to go camping in the mountains once or twice each year. We plan to go again next year, too.

Work with a partner. Read the model and answer the questions below.

1 How does the speaker begin the description? What is another way of starting the presentation?
2 Which sentence talks about the main subject of the photo?
3 What details does the speaker give about the friends? The view?
4 What are the friends doing? Which verb tense does the speaker use to explain this?
5 The speaker thinks it is a good photo. What reasons does he give?
6 What other detail(s) could the speaker give about the photo?
7 Look at the words *try* and *plan* in the last two sentences. What type of word follows them?

B Discuss

Discuss the questions with a partner.

1 Do you like the photo? Why or why not?
2 Is this a good or bad photo? Think of the tips you learned about on page 141.

Grammar

Gerunds and infinitives

Certain verbs can be followed by infinitives, and others can be followed by a gerund. Some verbs can be followed by either an infinitive or a gerund with little or no change in meaning. Study the forms:

Form	Verbs	Example
Verbs followed by infinitives verb + to + base form	*agree, expect, hope, need, plan, want, would like*	What do we need to know about our eyes?
Verbs followed by gerunds verb + ing	*enjoy, finish, suggest, try*	On clear nights we enjoy looking at the stars
Verbs followed by gerunds or infinitives verb + to + base form or verb + ing	*dislike, hate, like, love, prefer, start, try*	Stella prefers to study / prefers studying in the morning.

1   Choose the correct form to complete the restaurant description.

A good meal is an experience that includes many senses: taste, smell, touch, and sight. We enjoy [1] **to look / looking** at the colors, shapes, and design of the food on the plate. However, at one London restaurant, diners must enjoy their meal without their sense of sight because the dining room is totally dark. When the restaurant opened, the owners said they wanted [2] **to give / giving** people a new food experience. They also hoped [3] **to educate / educating** people about blindness. All the servers at the restaurant are blind. If you go to the restaurant, you should expect [4] **to leave / leaving** all sources of light, such as cell phones, or cameras, in another room. You might love [5] **to eat / eating** in the dark. Or you might hate it. Either way, it will be an adventure!

2   Complete the sentences with infinitives or gerunds and your own ideas.

1   On weekends, I hate _____.

2   Before I go to bed, I have to finish _____.

3   On vacation, I enjoy _____.

4   Before the end of the year, I plan _____.

5   I need to get more exercise. I would like to try _____.

3   Use the verbs in the Grammar box to make true or false sentences about yourself. Your classmates must guess if they are true or false.

Speaking skill

Use prepositions and prepositional phrases to describe the location of the subjects in a photo or picture.

Prepositions and Prepositional Phrases	Examples
in the background / foreground	*In the background, you can see Mount Jefferson.*
in front of / behind	*Here's my mother standing in front of her car.*
in the center / middle	*Marcus is the one in the middle with the blue jacket*
at the top / bottom of the picture	*There's a large rock at the bottom of the picture.*
on the right / left there is	*My brother is standing on the left.*
next to, near	*Robert is the one next to our blue tent*
above, between, over, under	*The photo shows a small dog hiding under a table.*

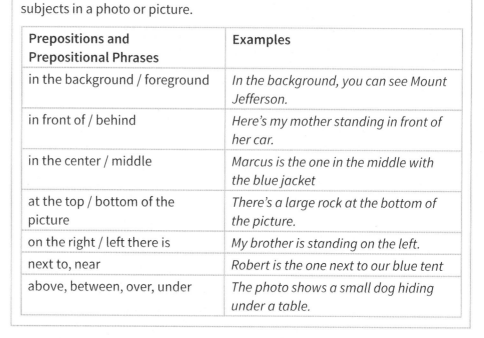

1 Look at the photo. Complete the description with words from the box.

> background   behind   between   left   next   right

This is a photo of a boy, his mother, and his father washing a red car. On the ¹_____, there is a red car. The boy and his mother are standing ²_____ to the car. The boy is washing the car with water and there is a bucket ³_____ the boy and the car. The father is ⁴_____ the boy and his mother. In the ⁵_____, there is a house and on the ⁶_____, there is a small garden. I really like this picture because the family is having fun and there is a nice shadow from the water on the side of the car.

2 Draw a picture scene in Box A. Then, describe the picture to your partner. Your partner must draw the picture in Box B. Use phrases for describing location.

Box A

Box B

Pronunciation for speaking

/p/ versus /b/

The sound /p/ as in *pin* is almost the same as the sound /b/ as in *bin*. The only difference is that /b/ is *voiced*. This means your vocal cords are vibrating. To pronounce /p/, touch your throat. Say /b/. You will feel vibration. Now, say /p/. Focus on the first sound. If you do it correctly, you will not feel any vibration.

1 Pronounce the words in the table below. Focus on your pronunciation of the /p/ sound.

1 put	4 portrait	7 position
2 pick	5 professional	8 place
3 perfect	6 picture	9 popular

2 Pronounce the words in the table below. Focus on your pronunciation of the /b/ sound.

1 big	4 boss	7 beautiful
2 best	5 blind	8 background
3 but	6 brother	9 balance

3 🎧 8.8 Pronounce the phrases in the table below. Focus on the difference between the /p/ and /b/ sound. Then listen and check your pronunciation.

1 a big place	4 a bright picture
2 a beautiful park	5 a popular bag
3 a professional boss	6 a perfect balance

Speaking task

Describe a photo. You must speak for at least 45 seconds.

Brainstorm

Choose one of the photos or a photo that you have taken yourself.
Study the photo and make notes about each topic in the box below.

> the subject   what's happening in the photo?   why is it a good photo?

Plan

Look back at your notes. Make an outline of the information you will include in your description. Include these parts:

1   Introduction: the subject of the photo; the date; and the place.
2   Body: talk about what's happening in the photo.
3   Conclusion: why it is a good photo? Why do you like it?

Look back at the speaking model on page 146 to help you. Remember to use phrases for describing location on page 148 and gerunds and infinitives on page 147.

Speak

Practice your description. Pay attention to your pronunciation of the /p/ and /b/ sounds.

Share

Describe your photo to your partner. Take turns asking and answering questions.

Reflect

Work in a small group and answer the question below.

What makes a good photograph?

Review

Wordlist

Vocabulary preview

background (n)***	landscape (n)**	shoot (v)***
blind (adj)**	notice (v)***	square (n)***
blink (v)*	photograph (n)***	twice (adv)***
degrees (n)***	position (n)***	view (n)***
depth (n)***	screen (n)***	vision (n)***
except (prep) ***	sense (n)***	

Vocabulary development

contrast (n)***	photographer (n)**	size (n)***
frame (n)**	picture (n)**	shadow (n)***
mood (n)***	scene (n)***	

Academic words

adults (n)***	complex (adj)***	location (n)***
called (adj)***	focus (v)***	professional (adj)***

Academic words review

Complete the sentences with the words in the box.

colleague	individual	location	obvious	series

1 She took a beautiful _____ of photos about her life in Vietnam.
2 My _____ and I have different views about caring for the environment at work.
3 The mountains are an excellent _____ to take some nice photos.
4 It is _____ when someone has taken a photo with a filter.
5 I have _____ computer files for every course I take at university.

Unit review

Listening 1	I can recognize numbers.
Listening 2	I can identify descriptive details.
Vocabulary	I can use words for talking about photos.
Grammar	I can use gerunds and infinitives.
Speaking	I can use phrases to describe location.
Pronunciation	I can pronounce /**p**/ and /**b**/ sounds.

9 PROGRESS

A changing world

Discussion point

Study the infographic and answer the questions.

1 How much has the total world population increased by from 2000 to present?

2 Are more or fewer people living in cities now than in 2000?

3 How many Internet users were there worldwide in 2000?

4 Is the worldwide temperature getting hotter or colder?

5 How many endangered species are there today?

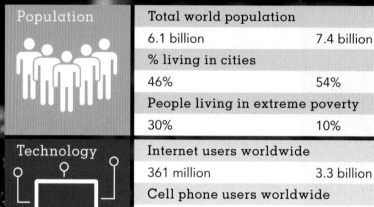

	2000	Present
Population	Total world population	
	6.1 billion	7.4 billion
	% living in cities	
	46%	54%
	People living in extreme poverty	
	30%	10%
Technology	Internet users worldwide	
	361 million	3.3 billion
	Cell phone users worldwide	
	8 per 100 people	80 per 100 people
	Newest car design	
	hybrid car	driverless car
Environment	Worldwide temperature	
	+0.4°C (vs. 1960)	+0.7°C (vs. 1960)
	Endangered species worldwide	
	11,043	16,928
	People killed by natural disasters	
	17,000	23,000

VIDEO

ROBOT WORKERS

Before you watch

Work with a partner. How can robots be used to help people in the following places?

1 at school _____

2 at work _____

3 in sport _____

4 at home _____

5 in a hospital _____

UNIT AIMS

LISTENING 1 Listening for past and present time signals
LISTENING 2 Listening for concluding phrases
STUDY SKILL Using technology to personalize learning

VOCABULARY Words to describe progress
GRAMMAR *Used to*
SPEAKING Ending a talk

Shibuya, Tokyo.

While you watch

Watch the video and mark the sentences *T* (True) or *F* (False).

1 The robot is designed to carry medical equipment. ——

2 The robot is the same size as an adult. ——

3 The robot needs help from the robot team to move around. ——

4 The robot can move around large objects, like people or furniture. ——

5 In the future, the robot will only be used in hospitals. ——

After you watch

Work with a partner. Design your own robot. Think about:

- How big is the robot?
- What can the robot do?
- How much does the robot cost?
- What does the robot look like?

Learning online

A Vocabulary preview

1 Read the sentences. Match the words in bold with the correct definition.

1 I play football every weekend and luckily, I have never had a serious **injury.**

2 I want to **improve** my grades so that I can study abroad.

3 I have an **efficient** way to learn a lot of English vocabulary so I can remember more words.

4 I am making a lot of **progress** in English this year. My exam score is much higher than the last one.

a _____ (v) make something better

b _____ (adj) working in a well-organized way that produces good results

c _____ (n) the process of getting better over a period of time

d _____ (n) pain or damage caused by an accident, e.g. in a sports game

5 My social life and hobbies don't **prevent** me from getting good grades in school.

6 The new **digital** cameras these days take beautiful pictures.

7 I still **keep in touch with** many of my friends from elementary school

8 My teachers are strict about deadlines, so I always **hand in** my assignments on time.

e _____ (v) stay in contact through phone, e-mail, letters, or social media

f _____ (adj) using or relating to computer technology

g _____ (v) to give a form or document to a person or organization

h _____ (v) to stop something from happening

2 Which of the sentences in Exercise 1 are true for you? Tell a partner.

B Before you listen

1 Look at the photographs. With a partner, describe what you can see.

In the first photograph, I can see …

In the second photograph, there is/are …

In the third photograph, a …is …

2 Think about your life ten years ago and five years ago. With a partner, talk about your life.

Ten years ago, I …   Five years ago, I …

C Global listening

 **9.1** Listen to two speakers talking about their online course. Choose the correct option to complete each sentence.

1 Anna talks about the differences between …

  a online classrooms and traditional classrooms.

  b high school and university.

  c print books and digital books.

2 Isabella likes the online course because she can …

  a send messages to her classmates.

  b ask questions and read lecture notes.

  c watch the lectures more than once.

3 Anna thinks that one of the advantages of taking an online course is that …

  a she can learn lots of different subjects.

  b it's easier to organize her study schedule.

  c she can learn from home.

4 … the disadvantages of taking an online course.

  a Anna talks about

  b Isabella talks about

  c Both Anna and Isabella talk about

5 Anna and Isabella finish the conversation by talking about …

  a the latest online lecture.

  b a newspaper article.

  c their plans for the weekend.

Listening for main ideas

GLOSSARY

assignment (n) a task or piece of work

distraction (n) something that stops you from studying or working

flexible (adj) able to change easily

Listening for past and present time signals

D Close listening

When speakers talk about the past and present in the same conversation or discussion, they often use specific words and phrases that can help you identify past and present time.

Past time signals: *when (back) then in the past in those days*

Present time signals: *now nowadays today these days*

🎧 **9.2** Listen to part of the conversation. Match the time expressions with the information they introduce.

1 In the past …
2 Now …
3 Back then …
4 Nowadays …
5 In those days …
6 These days …

a I used to run from one lecture room to another.
b we only used to discuss issues during the lectures.
c I can fit the online lectures around my timetable.
d we can ask questions and read lectures notes any time we like.
e I'm connected to the internet via my phone, tablet and even television.
f I used to send e-mails to my cousin in Australia.

E Critical thinking

Discuss the questions.

1 What are the advantages and disadvantages of taking an online course?
   One advantage/disadvantage of taking an online course is …
2 Do you think university courses will be completely online in the future?
   I don't think it will be necessary for students to go to a university building in the future …
   I think universities will continue to give courses in traditional classrooms …
3 Which university courses are not possible to learn online, in your opinion?
   I don't think it's possible to learn … online because …

Pronunciation for listening

Consonant clusters at the beginning and end of words

A consonant cluster is a group of two or more consonant sounds that are next to each other without a vowel between them. Many words in English begin or end with a consonant cluster:

Clusters at the beginning of words

stop,   **gr**eat,   **pl**ay

Clusters at the end of words

boo**ks**,   ha**nd**,   lo**st**

Practice listening for the consonant clusters at the beginning and end of words to help your understanding.

---

1 🎧 **9.3** Underline the consonant clusters at the beginning of these words. Then listen and notice the pronunciation.

> graduate   student   class   school   slide   progress   start

2 🎧 **9.4** Underline the consonant clusters at the end of these words. Then listen and notice the pronunciation.

> think   help   student   accept   sound   lift   past

3 🎧 **9.5** Listen and complete each word with the correct consonant cluster.

1 ___ ___ i n t	5 ___ ___ i l l	9 ___ ___ e s e n t
2 t h i ___ ___	6 a ___ ___	10 f a ___ ___
3 ___ ___ i e n d	7 ___ ___ a d e s	11 ___ ___ e p a r e
4 p r e v e ___ ___	8 p a t i e n ___ ___	12 i n s t a ___ ___

4 Write the missing word in each sentence. Underline the consonant cluster at the beginning or end of the word.

> change   conduct   different   friends   instant   patients

1 _____ can now survive for many years and live normally.

2 One positive change of all this technology is easy access to online _____ translators.

3 The way we communicate in general is also _____ now.

4 In the end, I guess _____ can be both positive and negative, but can't be stopped.

5 Many teachers these days _____ all of their lesson using presentation software.

6 I use social media to keep in touch with my _____.

Simon's new arm

A Vocabulary preview

1 Match the words in bold to the correct definition

   1 The roads are dangerous so I am worried about having an **accident** when I ride my bicycle.

   2 There are over 6,000 **objects** in the museum collection.

   3 It's easy to **attach** large documents to my e-mails on a smartphone.

   4 I can't **imagine** what life will be like in thirty years.

   5 When I was a **teenager**, I was the **star** soccer play at my school.

   a _____ (n) a person between the ages of thirteen and nineteen years old

   b _____ (adj) someone who is the best at something, e.g. a sport

   c _____ (v) connect or add one thing to another, e.g. a document to an e-mail

   d _____ (n) things that you can see and touch

   e _____ (v) form a picture or idea of something in your mind

   f _____ (n) a sudden event that is not planned, which causes pain or damage

2 Answer the questions with a partner.

   1 Are car accidents a problem in your country?

   2 Can you imagine what life will be like in thirty years?

   3 What sports did you play as a teenager? Were you a star?

   4 It is easy to attach large files on your smartphone?

   5 What object could you not live without?

B Before you listen

Activating prior knowledge

Look at the picture on page 159. Discus the questions with a partner.

1 How do you think the prosthetic arm works?

2 What kinds of actions do you think the arm can do?

3 How much do you think the prosthetic arm costs?

C Global listening

1 **9.6** Listen to *Simon's new arm*. Choose the topics the speaker talks about.

   ✓ When and how Simon lost his arm

   ___ The speaker's family

   ___ The speaker's activities as a teenager

   ___ How the prosthetic arm works

   ___ What Simon can do with the prosthetic arm

   ___ The speaker's future plans

   ___ The cost of the new prosthetic arm

   ___ The speaker's opinion about technology

D Close listening

1 **9.6** Listen again. Choose the best answer for each question.

1 How did Simon lose his arm?

  a from birth

  b a cycling accident at university

  c a disease as a child

2 What kind of activities did Simon do before he lost his arm?

  a tennis, basketball, swimming

  b running, baseball, volleyball

  c football, skiing, hiking

3 What can Simon do just by thinking?

  a raise his arm   b get dressed   c pick up an object

4 What can Simon do better than before his accident?

  a play tennis   b play golf   c play basketball

5 How much did Simon's prosthetic arm cost?

  a $35,000   b $45,000   c $55,000

6 How does Simon feel about his new arm?

  a disappointed   b satisfied   c very happy

Listening for main ideas

GLOSSARY

cutting-edge (adj) extremely modern and advanced

hold someone back (v) to stop someone from doing something

realistic (adj) an artificial object that looks natural

specialist (n) someone who is an expert in a particular subject

Listening for
concluding phrases

When people give a presentation, they will usually divide it into three different parts.
- Introduction
- Main body
- Conclusion

The conclusion comes at the end of a presentation. The purpose is to summarize the speaker's main ideas. The following signal phrases will help you to identify the conclusion.

In conclusion…   To sum up…   I'd like to summarize the main points…

2   🎧 **9.7** Listen to the final part of *Simon's new arm*. Which phrase does he use to conclude the presentation?

In conclusion… ☐   To sum up… ☐   I'd like to summarize the main points… ☐

E Critical thinking

Discuss the questions.

1   What surprised or interested you the most about Simon's talk? Why?

I was surprised that … I was interested to hear about …

2   What is your opinion of the prosthetic arm?

In my opinion …

3   Simon says that many people worry about the changes that modern technology brings. Do you worry about modern technology? Why?

I worry a lot/somewhat/a little about … because …

Study skills | Using technology to personalize learning

Some students prefer to work completely online; others prefer face-to-face learning; others a combination of both. Experiment to find the best combination for you. You may prefer, for example, to search for materials online, but read books in hard copy. You may find chat rooms useful for general discussion but prefer to meet face-to-face to prepare for a group presentation.

Taking part

- Once you have met group members and have a sense of what they are like, you may prefer to use social networking tools to contact them.

Keeping organized

- Keep an electronic diary. Set this to remind you of appointments.

Managing information

- You may prefer to take all your notes on a tablet device. However, you may find it more convenient, and easier to remember material, if you take notes by hand, especially in class.

Designing materials for assignments and revision

- Use video, photography, and drawing software to find ways of showing information that help you to make sense of it and to remember it.

© Stella Cottrell (2013)

1 Read the information about using technology to personalize learning. Then complete the table with check marks (✓) to show how you use technology to help you study.

Aspect of study / Technology	To keep myself organized	To work on group projects / activities	To learn from practice and feedback	To produce essays, talks, reports, etc.
Videos, photos, animations				
Course-based discussion board				
Online practice tests				
Social networking e.g. Facebook				
Podcasts				
Blogs				
Wikis				
Lecture chat				
Apps				

© Stella Cottrell (2013)

2 Write down two ways you will use technology to help you with your studies.

Vocabulary development

Words to describe progress

1 Read the sentences. Match the word in bold with the correct definition.

1 Antibiotics is possibly one of the best examples of modern **medicine**.
2 These days more people are shopping **online** rather than going to real stores.
3 **Access** to my school is difficult because there isn't a direct bus or train.
4 I must install some photo editing **software** on my new computer.
5 Computer software companies often ask users to suggest **improvements**.
6 Many people spend thousands of dollars a year on the most **up-to-date** technology.
7 It's faster to look up words on an **electronic** dictionary than in a print dictionary.
8 **Robots** can now do many jobs better and faster than humans.

a _____ (n) the programs and operating information used by a computer
b _____ (n) the study and practice of treating or preventing illnesses and injuries
c _____ (n) a way of going to or entering a place
d _____ (adj) connected to the internet or available through a computer network
e _____ (adj) using electricity and very small electrical parts
f _____ (n) something better than it was before
g _____ (n) machines that can perform tasks, often instead of humans
h _____ (adj) the most modern or latest version of something

2 Work with a partner. Answer the questions and explain your answers.

1 Do most people in your country have access to the internet?
2 Is it important for you to have the most up-to-date technology and software?
3 Are robots taking away people's jobs in your country?
4 What software programs on your computer do you use most often?
5 What do you usually buy online? Is there anything you wouldn't buy online?
6 What are the biggest improvements in medicine in your country?

Academic words

1 Choose the best definition for the word or phrase in bold.

1 This **file** is too large to send as an e-mail attachment.
   a a tool or instrument used for building something
   b a set of information or documents on a computer
   c a metal container to hold objects

2 My new internet connection is really fast, so I can download a complete video in a **couple** of minutes.
   a several   b many   c two

3 I really like to work in a **team** because you can share lots of interesting ideas.
   a one person   b a group of people   c an audience

4 There are so many choices to think about that it's difficult to make a **final** decision.
   a first or easy
   b the last or coming at the end
   c secret or silent

5 With **advanced** technology, I think we will have driverless cars very soon.
   a useful and practical
   b expensive and uncommon
   c new and developed

6 After a **brief** pause to answer a question, the scientist continued her lecture.
   a short   b very long   c quiet

2 Work with a partner. Answer the questions and explain your answers.

1 Are you good at organizing your files on your computer?

2 What couple of apps are the most important on your phone?

3 Do you prefer to work on your own or in a team when writing a presentation?

4 Do you often make brief pauses to think of the correct English grammar or vocabulary when you are speaking to someone?

5 How can advanced technology improve education?

6 Is it difficult for you to make a final decision about important things in your life?

Speaking model

You are going to learn about *used to* to talk about past habits, using concluding phrases and pronouncing stress for emphasis. You are then going to use these to talk about how life has changed in the last ten years.

A Analyze

Read the model and answer the questions below.

Good morning everyone. Today I'd like to talk about how life has changed in my country in the last ten years. My talk is divided into three parts. First, I'll talk about how communication has changed. Next, I'll talk about healthcare, and finally I'll talk about how education has changed.

In the past, people used to send a lot of letters. Now, people mainly communicate with friends and family via text messages and social media on their electronic devices, such as smartphones and tablets. One advantage of this is that communication is much faster than in the past. In my opinion, this is a positive change.

Next, let's think about healthcare. Hospitals are getting bigger and more advanced—with robots that can do surgery. In addition, people didn't use to know much about their own illness. Now people know more about diseases and medicine.

Finally, let's look at education. Education is becoming more and more digital. I used to have heavy print course books for all my classes and write all my notes on paper. Now, I use a tablet in the classroom and I save all my notes electronically.

In conclusion, I think these are positive changes. Communication is much faster than in the past. Healthcare is better and there is more technology to help people. I also think digital education is a good way to learn because we can access more information.

1 Number the topics in the order the speaker talks about them.

___ Communication   ___ Education   ___ Healthcare

2 According to the speaker, is communication on electronic devices positive or negative?

3 What two changes to hospitals does the speaker mention?

4 What does the speaker now use in the classroom?

5 In conclusion, is the speaker positive or negative about the changes?

B Discuss

Answer the questions with a partner.

1 What is the most important change the speaker talks about?

2 Do you agree with the speaker's conclusion about the changes?

Grammar

Used to

We use the expression *used to …* to talk about the difference between the past and now. For example:

- something we often did in the past but don't do now
- something that happened in the past, but doesn't happen anymore
- a situation that was different in the past from the way it is now

Notice the form of *used to + verb (inf)* in positive and negative statements, and in questions. The letter '*d*' is dropped from '*used to*' in negative statements and questions.

Positive: *I **used to** send e-mails to my cousin in Australia.*

Negative: *I **didn't use to** be a very good golfer.*

Question: ***Did** you **use to** study a lot in school?*

1 Complete the sentences with *used to*, *didn't use to* or *did use to.*

1 My home town is very big now. It _____ be much smaller.

2 There is so much traffic now but in the past there _____ be so many cars on the road.

3 _____ your father _____ play sports with you?

4 I grew up near my relatives, and we _____ visit them a lot.

5 What subject _____ you _____ like the most in elementary school?

6 My teachers _____ get angry at me because I always handed my homework in late.

2 Match the two sentence halves to form sentences.

1 I used to drive to work	a but now I go to a restaurant.
2 I used to live in a big city	b but now I take the bus.
3 Biology used to be my best subject	c but now it's crowded and noisy.
4 I used to eat lunch in my office	d but now I live in a small town.
5 I used to go out with my friends a lot	e but now I prefer Physics.
6 This city used to be quiet and peaceful	f but now I stay home and study.

3 Take it in turns to ask and answer the questions below with a partner.

10 years ago	Now
Where did you use to live?	Where do you live now?
What hobbies did you use to have?	What hobbies do you have now?
What food did you use to enjoy eating?	What food do you enjoy eating now?
What music did you use to listen to?	What music do you listen to now?

Speaking skill

It is important to structure the end of your presentation so that the audience knows that you are finished and you are ready to answer questions. The end of a presentation can include the following points:
- Bringing a presentation to an end
- Thanking the audience
- Inviting questions

1 Write the phrases in the box under the correct headings.

> That brings me to the end of my presentation.
> Does anyone have any questions? Thank you very much for listening.
> I'll be happy to answer any questions. That concludes my talk.
> Thank you for your attention.

Bringing a presentation to an end

_____

_____

Thanking the audience

_____

_____

Inviting questions

_____

_____

2 Read the conclusion below. Choose one phrase from each category in Exercise 1 and write them in the space below to end the presentation.

> *In conclusion, these are positive changes. Communication is much faster than in the past. Healthcare is better and there is more technology to help people, for example the prosthetic arm. I also think digital education is a good way to learn because we have more software.* _____
>
> _____
>
> _____.

3 Write one question you can ask at the end of the presentation.

4 Take turns ending the presentation. Ask your partner your question from Exercise 3.

Pronunciation for speaking

Stress for emphasis

We can stress a particular word or phrase in a sentence by saying it louder, and making the vowel sound longer. This tells the listener that the stressed word carries the most important point in the sentence. Notice the words that are stressed in the sentence.

I **used to** drink tea in the morning.	(Not now)
I used to drink **tea** in the morning.	(Not coffee or milk)
I used to drink tea in the **morning**.	(Not in the afternoon or evening)

1 🎧 9.8 Listen to each recording of the sentence below. Underline the word that is stressed in each sentence.

   a I used to sleep ten hours a day when I was a child.

   b I used to sleep ten hours a day when I was a child.

   c I used to sleep ten hours a day when I was a child.

2 Write the letter of the sentence in Exercise 1 that matches the emphasized point below.

   1 ___ not six or eight hours a day

   2 ___ not when I was a baby or a teenager

   3 ___ not play or study

3 Work with a partner. Practice saying the sentences. Stress the important information.

   1 I used to live in a city.   (not a town or village)

   2 English used to be my worst subject.   (not Science or Math)

   3 My mother used to take me to school.   (not my father or brother)

   4 I used to be a terrible singer.   (not great or average)

   5 I used to study for four hours every night.   (not two or three hours)

Speaking task

Describe how life has changed in the last ten years. You must speak for at least one minute.

Brainstorm

Choose four topics from the box and write them into the first column of the table below.

> Family life   Study   Friends   Interests   Education
> Healthcare   Technology   Communication

Topic	Ten years ago	Now
Topic 1:		
Topic 2:		
Topic 3:		
Topic 4:		

Plan

Look at the topics in the first column. Think of one example of how each of these used to be different ten years ago. Write your examples in the second column. Remember to use the phrase *used to*.

Work with a partner. Look at your examples in the second column. Write how these have changed. Write your ideas in the third column. Use the present simple or present progressive form (see Unit 4).

Speak

Plan and write your talk. Remember to include an introduction and a conclusion. Look back at page 94 for phrases for making an introduction and page 160 for phrases for making a conclusion.

Share

Work with a partner. Take it in turns to give your talks. Remember to use emphasis in sentences with *used to*.

Reflect

Work in a group. How much has life changed in the last ten years? Give reasons to support your answers.

Review

Wordlist

MACMILLAN DICTIONARY

Vocabulary preview

accident (n)***	imagine (v)***	object (n)***
attach (v)**	improve (v)***	prevent (v)***
digital (adj)**	injury (n)***	progress (n)***
efficient (adj)***	keep in touch with (phrase)	star (n)***
hand in (v)		teenager (n) **

Vocabulary development

access (n)***	medicine (n)**	software (n)***
electronic (adj)***	online (adj)**	up-to-date (adj)*
improvement (n)***	robots (n)*	

Academic words

advanced (adj)***	couple (n)***	final (adj)***
brief (adj)***	file (n)***	team (n) ***

Academic words review

Complete the sentences with the words in the box.

> advanced   channel   complex   location   method

1   There is a gym, supermarket, and restaurant all in one _____. It's so convenient.
2   I try to read _____ academic English texts to improve my understanding of difficult words.
3   My tennis improved when I tried a new _____ of serving.
4   Computers have become very _____ and can do a lot.
5   The TV _____ I usually watch is only available online.

Unit review

Listening 1	☐	I can listen for past and present time signals.
Listening 2	☐	I can listen for concluding phrases.
Vocabulary	☐	I can use words to describe progress.
Grammar	☐	I can use *used to* to talk about past events.
Speaking	☐	I can use phrases to end a talk.
Pronunciation	☐	I can put stress into sentences with *used to*.

J⚙bs in the U.S.A.

Discussion point

Study the infographic and answer the questions.

1 Which job will increase the most between 2014 and 2024?

2 Which job will decrease the most between 2014 and 2024?

3 Why do you think the five jobs in the infographic will increase or decrease by 2024?

4 What information in the chart surprised you?

5 Do you think the information is the same or different in your country?

Job	2014	2024	% Change	Average Salary
Car park ticket inspector	9,400	7,400	-20.8	$36,530
Computer programmer	328,600	302,200	-8.0	$79,530
Fast food cook	524,400	444,000	-15.3	$19,080
Lawyer	778,700	822,500	5.6	$115,820
Nurse	2,751,000	3,190,000	16	$67,490

VIDEO

DRIVERLESS TAXI

Before you watch

Work with a partner. Discuss the questions.

1 Can you imagine being in a car with no driver? How would you feel?

2 What can a driverless car do better than a human driver?

3 What are the good and bad points about making a whole city use driverless cars?

UNIT
AIMS

LISTENING 1 Listening for additional information
LISTENING 2 Reviewing parts of a talk
STUDY SKILL Combining work and study

VOCABULARY Words for talking about work
GRAMMAR Future with *will*
SPEAKING Using future time markers

A robot vacuuming.

While you watch

1   Predict which one word you will hear in the video to complete the sentence.

 1   You can call a taxi using an _____ on your phone.

 2   An engineer from the company that designs the cars must _____ the car before the public can use them.

 3   The car waits when _____ or objects go in front of it to stop accidents.

 4   The car will change how _____ are built in the future.

2   Watch the video and check your answers.

After you watch

Work with a partner. Discuss the questions.

1   Would you be happy to sit in a driverless car? Why? / Why not?

   I would / wouldn't be happy to sit in a driverless car because …

2   What problems might there be with driverless cars and taxis?

   One problem might be …

3   The engineer says how driverless cars will change cities. What other changes do you predict?

   I think there might be other changes such as …

Love your job

A Vocabulary preview

1 Match the words in bold with the correct definition.

1	**unusual** (adj)	a	paintings, drawing, sculptures etc.
2	**check** (v)	b	not normal, common or typical
3	**art** (n)	c	to do an activity
4	**take part** (v)	d	to study something to make sure it is correct
5	**review** (n)	e	to repair something that is broken
6	**fix** (v)	f	a group of things, or ideas that are all different from one another
7	**sell** (v)	g	someone's opinion, e.g. of a book, movie, or restaurant
8	**variety** (n)	h	to exchange something for money

2 Complete the sentences below with the words in bold from Exercise 1.

1 I like to _____ in social activities such as sports and movie clubs.

2 I'd like to have an _____ job in the future, like a chocolate taster.

3 I _____ my phone for updates every minute. My friend thinks it's too much.

4 I really enjoy visiting _____ galleries and museums.

5 A lot of my friends buy and _____ things online but I prefer going to shops.

6 I can _____ problems with my computer. I don't need to ask for help.

7 I like shopping in big supermarkets because there is so much _____.

8 I will not eat at a restaurant if my friends give it a negative _____.

3 Work with a partner. Which of the sentences are true for you?

B Before you listen

Discuss with a partner.

Activating prior knowledge

1 What are the most important characteristics of a job? Look at the list and choose the three you think are most important. Compare with a partner.

- high salary
- helping others
- working in another country
- good colleagues
- well-known company
- a fun atmosphere
- lots of variety
- a company car

2 What is your dream job? Discuss with a partner.

3 Look at the two jobs on page 173. What do you think each person does?

C Global listening

1 🎧 **10.1** You are going to listen to a chocolate consultant and a car test driver talking about their jobs. Predict who will say these words. Write *CC* (chocolate consultant) or *TD* (test driver). Then listen to *Love your job* and check your predictions.

1	eat chocolate	4	safety features
2	deal with restaurants	5	one disadvantage is related to health
3	performance of cars	6	a lot of concentration

2 🎧 **10.1** Listen again and choose three facts each speaker gives.

1 **Alexandra: Chocolate consultant**

a She has a university degree in food engineering.

b A chocolate consultant studies the art of making chocolate.

c She gives advice to people who make chocolate.

d She eats about 1 kg of chocolate every week.

e She may need to find a new job in the future.

2 **Steven: Test driver**

a He tests the performance of cars.

b He works with racing drivers.

c He studies charts, graphs, and computer models.

d He helps to make cars safer.

e He tests driverless cars.

Predicting

GLOSSARY

concentration (n) the process of paying close attention to something

consultant (n) a person with specialist knowledge who can give advice

manufacturer (n) a company that makes a product

performance (n) how fast or well something works

Chocolate consultant

Test driver

D Close listening

Listening for
additional information

> When speakers give a series of facts, ideas, or opinions, they often use
> signal words and expressions to add extra information. Listen for these
> signals to help you identify the items that the speaker adds:
>
> *above all, additionally, as well (as), most of all, in addition, most importantly,
> on top of that, that's not all.*

1　🎧 **10.2** Listen to excerpts from *Love your job*. Match the expressions with
the important items.

1	Above all	a	I enjoy is taking part in chocolate tasting events
2	Another thing	b	I love working with chocolate makers
3	In addition	c	I feel like I'm doing something useful
4	That's not all	d	we study charts, graphs and computer models
5	Most of all	e	I also deal with restaurants and retail stores

2　🎧 **10.3** Listen and complete the sentences. Then underline the additional
information.

1　As a university professor, I teach classes three days a week. But
_____ I do. I also prepare lectures, correct students'
homework, and attend meetings.

2　In my job I write sales reports, order supplies, and _____,
visit my customers.

3　I am so busy this week. I have two exams, three reports to write, a meeting
with my English professor, and _____, I have to work
every night at the restaurant.

4　What do I love about my job? Let me see… my work is really interesting, I have
weekends free, my office is near my home, and _____, my
colleagues are very friendly.

E Critical thinking

Discuss the questions.

1　Which job from *Love your job* sounds more interesting?

2　What three questions would you ask the guest speakers about their jobs?
Think about: *pay, qualifications, satisfaction, travel, working hours*

3　How will the jobs of chocolate taster and test driver change in the future?

Study skills Combining work and study

Many students work and study at the same time. For example:

- full-time workers who study part-time
- full-time students who do home-based work, such as child care
- full-time students who need to work for money or to help with a family business.

Benefits of working while studying

Getting experience and skills

Becoming more confident in work situations

Becoming more adult and independent

Learning about different professions and businesses

Understanding how classroom learning is used in professional practice

Earning money

Meeting people who can help you in your career

© Stella Cottrell (2013)

1 Work with a partner. Discuss the questions.

  1 Have you ever had a job?

  2 In your country, is it common for students to have jobs?

  3 What are the most popular jobs for students?

2 With your partner, read the following descriptions of students. Choose the three most important benefits of working while studying from the box for each student.

> **Student A:** Camilla, 18 years old, first-year student. She is not sure which major to choose. Her parents and most of their friends are artists, so she does not know much about other professions. She is shy and has never had a job.

> **Student B:** Elizabeth, 19 years old, second-year student. She is the oldest daughter in a big family. Her parents do not earn much money. Her major is nursing, but she has no experience taking care of sick people, and she worries that she will not make enough money as a nurse. She is thinking about changing her major to business.

> **Student C:** Mateo, 20 years old, third-year law student. He is an excellent student but doesn't know if the material in his classes is useful in the real world. He lives at home and his parents take care of everything he needs. He would like to be more independent.

The future of work

A Vocabulary preview

1 Match the words in bold with the correct definition.

1	**century** (n)	a	probably going to happen, or probably true
2	**designers** (n)	b	a person who makes the decisions in a company
3	**disappear** (v)	c	jobs that require special training, skill, or education
4	**likely** (adj)	d	a period of 100 years
5	**professions** (n)	e	people who plan how something will look or function
6	**boss** (n)	f	to become impossible to see; stop existing

2 Complete the predictions with words in bold from Exercise 1.

1 In the next ten years there will be a decreasing demand for graphic _____.

2 It is _____ that we will need more psychologists in the future.

3 As drones become more common, the job of a pizza delivery person will _____.

4 By the middle of the 21st _____, humans will live permanently on Mars.

5 By the year 2025, most _____ will require only a high-school education.

6 More people will be independent workers, so each person will be his or her own _____.

3 Work with a partner. Read the predictions in Exercise 2. Do you think they are true or false?

B Before you listen

Activating prior knowledge

Read the list of predictions about the future of work in the table below and check (✓) the box that matches your opinion.

	very likely	likely	unlikely	very unlikely
Robots will replace humans in factories.				
Robots will replace teachers.				
Offices will no longer exist because everyone will work from home.				
Today's young workers will have at least 15 jobs in their lives.				
Most people will continue working until the age of 75 or older.				

C Global listening

1 🎧 **10.4** Listen to *The future of work* and number these topics in order.

___ How jobs will change in the future

___ The number of freelancers

_1_ Artificial intelligence

___ Disadvantages of telecommuting

___ Freelance economy

___ Working from home

> A presentation or talk is often divided into three parts:
>
> **Introduction**: Introduce your topic, and outline the structure.
>
> **Body**: Talk about the advantages and disadvantages, steps in a process, facts and opinions, explanations, examples, descriptive details, cause and effects, and sequencers.
>
> **Conclusion**: In this part you summarize your ideas and say your final thoughts. For example, you can make predictions about the future.

Reviewing the parts of a talk

2 🎧 **10.5** Listen to excerpts from the lecture. Fill in the missing words.

1 Today we're going to move into the future, and _____ three developments that will change the way people work.

2 The first and most important development is artificial intelligence. _____ that computers will have the ability to think.

3 Some of these changes will be positive. _____, boring or dangerous jobs will be done by robots.

4 Soon we'll probably have driverless taxis. _____, there won't be any more need for human taxi drivers.

5 All right, moving on, the _____ important trend I want to mention is the growth of the freelance economy.

6 One _____, however, will be the loss of security and benefits.

7 This trend has huge _____, both for employers and for workers.

8 So, _____, I've presented three of the most important trends that are going to change the way people work in the future.

3 Match the sentence number in Exercise 2 with the part of the talk below.

Advantage ___   Introduction _1_   Talk about cause and effect ___

Conclusion ___   Give an explanation ___   Use sequencers ___

Disadvantage ___   Give an example ___

GLOSSARY

artificial intelligence (n) the use of computer technology to do tasks that people can do

freelancer (n) someone who works for themselves and sells their services to more than one company

flexibility (n) the ability to make changes or deal with a changing situation

telecommute (v) to work in a location, often one's home, that is not the employer's workplace.

Listening for details

D Close listening

1 🎧 10.6 Listen to Part 2 of the lecture. Which advantage of working as a freelancer does the speaker mention?

   a Freelancers have more flexibility.

   b Employers can save money because offices will be smaller.

   c Workers get excellent benefits.

   d Salaries are higher.

2 🎧 10.7 Listen to Part 3 of the lecture. Which disadvantage of telecommuting does the speaker mention?

   a Workers are not good at managing their own time.

   b Workers may have trouble separating their work life and their home life.

   c Managers can't supervise their employees.

   d Workers still have to travel to an office once or twice a week.

E Critical thinking

Discuss the questions.

1 The speaker discussed four ways that jobs will change in the future. Here is a list of additional predictions. Work with a partner. Choose the three trends that you think will be the most important in the next 10–20 years. Discuss why they will be important.

---

1. The end of retirement—people will keep working into old age.

2. People will live longer and longer.

3. Alternative sources of energy, e.g. solar and wind, will become more popular.

4. The Internet of Things – all objects will be able to send and receive data

5. People will have many jobs and many careers in their lives.

6. Your idea: _____

---

2 Which trend will have the greatest effect on your future job or profession? Why?

3 Which jobs will probably not change very much in the next 10–20 years? Why?

Pronunciation for listening

Silent syllables

In spoken English, we don't always pronounce every letter of every word. For example, the word *interesting* sometimes has a silent *e* in the middle of the word when spoken.

We write: *interesting*
We say: ˈɪntrəstɪŋ

Notice how the first letter *e* is not pronounced.

It's important to notice which letters are pronounced and which are silent in order to say and understand the word correctly.

1 🎧 **10.8** Listen to the following words and notice the silent letter. Then listen again and repeat.

1	interesting	5	average
2	temperature	6	comfortable
3	camera	7	useful
4	separate	8	several

2 Look at the underlined word in each sentence below. Circle the silent letter.

1 I'd like to introduce our first guest, Alexandra Green, who is a <u>chocolate</u> consultant.

2 First of all, I'm really <u>interested</u> in chocolate.

3 Now let's hear about a very <u>different</u> job.

4 It's important to check all the <u>safety</u> features.

5 I'm part of a team that tests the performance of cars to make sure they're <u>completely</u> safe.

3 Work with a partner. Take turns reading the sentences in Exercise 2 with the correct pronunciation of the underlined words.

Vocabulary development

Words for talking about work

1 Read the sentences. Match the words in bold with the correct definition.

1 It's important for me to have a job with a high **salary** so that I can support my family.

2 June wants to be a journalist, but she's worried that she won't **earn** much money.

3 In the future there will be an extremely high **demand** for people with good computer and writing skills.

4 I don't want a job in an **office**. I'd like to work outside.

5 Because of her excellent performance, Janet was chosen as **employee** of the month.

6 In a 2016 survey, people said Marathon Petroleum was the best **employer** in the United States.

7 In the past, most people had only one **career** for their whole lives.

8 A home health worker **takes care of** sick or elderly people at home.

a _____ (v) to receive money for work you do

b _____ (n) a room or building where people work

c _____ (n) the amount of money that a job pays

d _____ (n) the amount of a product or service that people want

e _____ (v) to look after someone or something

f _____ (n) a worker

g _____ (n) a job or series of jobs someone does in their working life

h _____ (n) a manager or boss; company to work for

2 Discuss the questions with a partner.

1 Is it more important to you to earn a lot of money or to have a job you love?

2 What is an average salary for a doctor in your country?

3 In companies in your country, is there a high demand for people who speak English?

4 In your country, who takes care of elderly people?

5 Would you prefer to be an employee or an employer? Why?

6 How many careers did your parents have? Is this number typical in your culture?

7 Where would you like to work? Would you be happy working in an office?

Academic words

1 Complete the definitions with the words in the box. Use a dictionary to help you.

| author conference contract involve project security |

1 _____ (n) a work agreement between an employer and employee

2 _____ (n) someone who writes books, articles, etc. as a job

3 _____ (n) a large meeting, sometimes lasting several days

4 _____ (n) a planned piece of work that has a goal or purpose

5 _____ (v) to include

6 _____ (n) safety from attack or harm

2 Complete the questions with the words and phrases from Exercise 1.

1 Would you like to be an _____ in the future? Why / Why not?

2 Do you have a hobby? What skills does it _____?

3 When you have to complete a _____, do you like to work alone or with others?

4 Why do people usually go to a _____?

5 Would you prefer to have a full-time or a freelance _____ in the future?

6 How can companies protect the _____ of their private data and information?

3 Work with a partner. Ask and answer the questions in Exercise 2.

Speaking model

You are going to learn about future forms, using future time markers, and pronouncing contractions with *will*. You will then use these to give a talk about a job that will change in the future.

A Analyze

Read the model and complete the outline below with the correct information.

Hi, I'm Charlotte. Welcome to my talk about jobs of the future. Today, I'd like to talk about the job of nursing. I've divided my talk into two parts. First I'll talk about nursing today. Then I'll make some predictions about the future of this job. To begin, a registered nurse is responsible for taking care of patients in a hospital. In the United States this job requires a bachelor's degree, which is a high level of education. According to my research there were about 2,751,000 jobs for registered nurses in the United States in 2015. I predict that the number of nurses will grow because people are living longer and longer. We'll have a larger number of old people, and they will most likely need more care. For the same reason, I predict that the salary for registered nurses will increase in the future. Today registered nurses in the U.S. earn an average of $67,490 a year. I think this salary will definitely grow. My third prediction is that more and more nurses will be freelancers. Because there will be a high demand for this job, nurses will probably be able to choose where and when they work. In conclusion, I think nursing will continue to be an excellent profession in the future.

Job: [1]	
Job responsibilities: [2]	
Education: [3]	
Number of jobs in 2015: [4]	Salary: [5]
Three predictions about nursing in the future:	
[6]	
[7]	
[8]	
Conclusion: [9]	

B Discuss

Work with a partner. Discuss the questions.

1 Which three jobs will become more popular in the next ten years? Which three jobs will become less popular?

2 What job would you like to have ten years from now?

Grammar

Future with *will*

We can use *will/won't* + verb to talk about actions and events in the future. We can add the words *definitely* (100%), *most likely* (80–90%), or *probably* (70–80%) to say how sure we are that something will happen.

I think this salary will definitely grow.
They will most likely need more care.
Nurses will probably be able to choose where they work.

Notice that *definitely*, *most likely*, and *probably*, come <u>after</u> *will* in positive statements. In negative statements, *definitely*, *most likely*, and *probably* come <u>before</u> *won't*.

---

1 Read the information about disappearing jobs. Underline the future forms. Highlight *definitely, most likely,* or *probably.*

Many professions will grow in the next 20 years, but others will most likely disappear. For example, mail carriers probably won't exist 20 years from now. This job will disappear because we won't need people to deliver the mail to our homes anymore. That's because we will most likely use less paper in the future. Also, 20 years from now, machines will perform many jobs that are done by humans today. For example, some companies are using small flying machines called drones that will deliver packages in 30 minutes or less. Within 20 years, these unmanned, flying machines will definitely replace today's human mail carriers.

2 Complete the predictions using *will* or *won't* and one of the verbs in the box.

be able   decrease   disappear   have   replace   ~~take place~~

1 In the future, most job interviews __will take place__ via video conferencing.
2 Surgeons _____ the chance to add memory to a human brain.
3 Computers _____ to do every job that humans can do today.
4 The number of travel agents _____ because people will use the internet more and more to plan their own trips.
5 Paper textbooks _____ because classrooms will be online.
6 Robots _____ human workers at fast-food restaurants.

3 Look at the topics. How will they change in the future?

work   travel   health   sport   communication

Speaking skill

When you are predicting future developments and trends, use expressions like *in the future*, *soon*, *in the next…*, and *…years from now* to signal that you are talking about the future.

In the future, offices will not use printers, because they will no longer use paper.

Soon, there will be large numbers of driverless taxis on the roads.

In the next ten years, more and more students will earn a degree by taking all their courses online.

Twenty years from now, most fast-food workers will be robots.

Note: Most often these time markers appear at the beginning of a sentence, but they can also go in the middle or at the end.

Offices will not use printers <u>in the future</u> because they will no longer use paper.

Robots will work in fast-food restaurants <u>ten years from now</u>.

1 Add the time markers in parentheses to the sentences. Place them at the beginning, middle, or end. Compare answers with a partner.

1 I think the local job market for college graduates will improve. (In the next ten years)

_____

2 I think the number of eco-friendly companies will expand. (Soon)

_____

3 Experts think that many low-tech jobs will disappear. (In the next 20 years)

_____

4 It is clear that new career areas will be developed. (In the future)

_____

5 Do you think that most workers will need to speak English? (Fifty years from now)

_____

2 Work with a partner. Use the time markers to make three more predictions about your life in the future. Place the time markers at the beginning, middle, or end of your prediction.

| in the future | in fifty years | in the next ten years | soon | twenty years from now |

In the next ten years, I will be married / I will be married in the next ten years.

Pronunciation for speaking

Pronouncing contractions with *will*

In natural speech, speakers usually contract *will* and *will not* as follows:

Affirmative		*Negative*	
I'll	*I'll see you later.*	I	*I won't see you later.*
You'll	*You'll need a computer.*	You	*You won't need a computer.*
He'll	*He'll rent a car.*	He	*He won't rent a car.*
She'll	*She'll be at the meeting.*	She	*She won't be at the meeting.*
It'll	*It'll be easy.*	It	*It won't be easy.*
We'll	*We'll follow you.*	We	*We won't follow you.*
They'll	*They'll fix the mistake.*	They	*They won't fix the mistake.*

Note: In affirmative statements, stress the verb following the contraction:
I'll **wait** for you.
In negative statements, stress both the contraction and the verb:
I **won't wait** for you.

1 🎧 **10.9** Listen and complete the sentences with contractions. Then listen again and repeat.

1 _____ need a coat.   7 _____ be home later.

2 _____ graduate in June.   8 _____ need the car tonight.

3 _____ have enough time.   9 _____ be OK.

4 _____ buy a car.   10 _____ see you later.

5 _____ pay for dinner.   11 _____ be at the office.

6 _____ be late.   12 _____ be a problem.

2 Work with a partner. Make affirmative and negative predictions about the people in parentheses. Use pronouns and contractions.

In five years …

In five years, I'll be an engineer. I won't be a student.

1 (You)

2 (Your partner)

3 (You and your family)

4 (The job market in your country)

Speaking task

Talk about a job and make predictions about how it will change in the future. You must speak for at least one minute.

Brainstorm

Pick a job or profession that interests you and that you know something about. You may also choose one of the jobs from the infographic on page 170. Use the chart to take notes about the job. Use the trends on page 184 to make predictions.

Description	Job: _____
Job role	
Education	
Salary	
Other details	
Prediction 1	
Prediction 2	
Prediction 3	

Plan

Outline your talk. Use the model on page 182 and the points below to help you.

- Additional signals (page 174)
- The parts of a talk (page 177)
- Future with *will* (page 183)
- Future time markers (page 184)

Speak

Practice your talk. Pay attention to your pronunciation of future forms and your use of future time markers.

Share

Give your talk and answer your classmates' questions.

Reflect

Work with a small group. Answer the question.

How will jobs change in the future?

Review

Wordlist

MACMILLAN
DICTIONARY

Vocabulary Preview

art (n)***	disappear (v)***	sell (v)***
boss (n)***	fix (v)***	take part (v)
century (n)***	likely (adj) ***	unusual (adj)***
check (v)***	professions (n)***	variety (n)***
designers (n)**	review (n)***	

Vocabulary development

career (n)***	employee (n)***	salary (n)**
demand (n)***	employer (n)***	take care (v)
earn (v)***	office (n)***	

Academic words

author (n)***	contract (n)***	project (n)***
conference (n)***	involve (v)***	security (n)***

Academic words review

Complete the sentences with the words in the box.

author	files	colleagues	normal	transportation

1 I have really nice _____ at work. We all get on really well.
2 Public _____, like trains and buses, is really good in my city.
3 It is _____ to greet a colleague by their surname in Germany.
4 An _____ is someone who writes books.
5 I keep all of my important _____ on my computer and on a memory stick.

Unit review

Listening 1	☐	I can listen for additional information.
Listening 2	☐	I can understand the different parts of a talk.
Vocabulary	☐	I can use words to talk about work.
Grammar	☐	I can use *will* to make predictions about the future.
Speaking	☐	I can use future time markers.
Pronunciation	☐	I can pronounce contractions with *will*.

Student role cards

Unit 5, Speaking task, page 96

	Chile	Norway	Malaysia
Greetings	1 Men shake hands 2 Women kiss on cheek 3 Greet by time of day: Buenos diás = good morning Buenos tardes = Good afternoon Buenos noches = good evening	1 Shake hands with everyone: men, women, children 2 OK to use first name with people you meet	1 Shake hands with men 2 Nod head or bow to women 3 Introduce most important or eldest person first
Attitude to time	1 Business meeting: arrive on time 2 Meeting with friends: OK to arrive 15–30 mins late	1 Arrive five mins early for business meetings 2 Be on time for social events	1 It's OK to be a little late for meetings
Dining	1 Keep hands above the table 2 Eat everything on your plate	1 Hold fork in left hand and knife in right hand 2 Put knife and fork across center of plate when finished	1 Don't use left hand to eat 2 Offer and accept drinks with both hands 3 In restaurant allow host to order all dishes
Gift giving	1 Bring flowers to host 2 Don't give yellow, black or purple flowers 3 Open gift immediately after receiving it	1 Bring flowers, chocolates, or cake to someone's home 2 Don't give even number of flowers 3 Open gift immediately after receiving it	1 Give pastries or chocolates to host 2 Don't wrap gifts in white or yellow paper 3 Don't open gift in front of guest

Unit 6, Speaking task, page 114

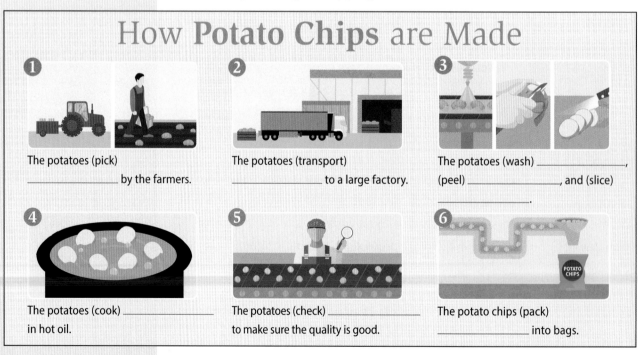

How **Potato Chips** are Made

1 The potatoes (pick) _____ by the farmers.

2 The potatoes (transport) _____ to a large factory.

3 The potatoes (wash) _____, (peel) _____, and (slice) _____.

4 The potatoes (cook) _____ in hot oil.

5 The potatoes (check) _____ to make sure the quality is good.

6 The potato chips (pack) _____ into bags.

Functional language phrase bank

The phrases below give common ways of expressing useful functions. Use them to help you as you're completing the *Discussion points, Critical thinking* activities, and *Speaking* tasks.

Asking for clarification
Sorry, can you explain that some more?
Could you say that another way?
When you say … do you mean …?
Sorry, I don't follow that.
What do you mean?

Asking for repetition
Could you repeat that, please?
I'm sorry, I didn't catch that.
Could you say that again?

When you don't know the word for something
What does … mean?
Sorry, I'm not sure what … means.

Working with a partner
Would you like to start?
Shall I go first?
Shall we do this one first?
Where do you want to begin?

Giving opinions
I think that …
It seems to me that …
In my opinion …
As I see it …

Agreeing and disagreeing
I know what you mean.
That's true.
You have a point there.
Yes. I see what you're saying, but …
I understand your point, but …
I don't think that's true.

Asking for opinions
Do you think …?
Do you feel …?
What do you think about …?
How about you, Jennifer?
What do you think?
What about you?
Does anyone have any other ideas?
Do you have any thoughts on this?

Asking for more information
In what way?
Why do you think that?
Can you give an example?

Not giving a strong preference
It doesn't matter to me.
I don't really have a strong preference.
I've never really thought about that.
Either is fine.

Expressing interest
I'd like to hear more about that.
That sounds interesting.
How interesting!
Tell me more about that.

Giving reasons
This is … because …
This has to be … because …
I think … because …

Checking understanding
Do you know what I mean?
Do you see what I'm saying?
Are you following me?

Putting things in order
This needs to come first because …
I think this is the most/least important because …
For me, this is the most/least relevant because …

Academic words revision

Units 1–5

Complete the sentences using the words in the box.

area available believe contact culture enormous
environment grades uniform volunteer

1 I don't _____ that birth order has an effect on your personality.
2 He's a model student. He arrives on time and gets good _____.
3 Taking your shoes off to enter a house is an important part of my
   _____.
4 My brother works as a _____ for a charity in Africa.
5 Walking to work is good for the _____.
6 Sadly, we don't have any apartments _____ at the moment.
7 Ginza is a busy shopping _____ in the south of Tokyo.
8 Her house is _____. It has 15 bedrooms!
9 It's unusual for students in the U.S.A. to wear a _____.
10 I've lost _____ with a lot of the people I went to school with.

Units 6–10

Complete the sentences using the words in the box.

accurate author contract final location percent
professional series system team

1 Only about 2.6 _____ of adults in the U.K. never eat meat.
2 Dr. Lindgren is giving a _____ of lectures on the effects of sugar.
3 Many believe that Seoul has the best transportation _____ in
   the world.
4 It's important that all the information in this report is _____.
5 My sister wants to be a _____ photographer in the future.
6 Lake Clark in Alaska is a popular _____ for nature photographers.
7 We need to make a _____ decision about this and finish the project.
8 Earlier this year, a _____ of scientists built the world's most
   accurate clock.
9 Carl Sagan was the _____ of many books on astronomy.
10 I have to sign a new _____ for my new job.

Macmillan Education
4 Crinan Street
London N1 9XW
A division of Macmillan Publishers Limited

Companies and representatives throughout the world

ISBN 978-1-786-32355-2

Written by Lida Baker and Steven Gershon
Series Consultant Dorothy E. Zemach

This edition published 2018

First edition entitled "Skillful" published 2012 by Macmillan Publishers Limited

Designed by emc design ltd
Illustrated by emc design ltd
Cover design by emc design ltd
Cover picture by Sam Parij (Eye Candy Illustration)/Getty Images/ Moment Open/Alicia Llop
Picture research by Julie-anne Wilce

Authors' acknowledgements

Lida Baker
I would like to thank my husband, Paul Nisenbaum, for his endless patience and support. This book is dedicated to him and to my daughter, Galya.

Steven Gershon
Heartfelt appreciation to my students and ELT colleagues, who never fail to provide the inspiration, ideas and tools I need to make the classroom a lively, active, engaging educational environment. Special thanks also to Britt for always lending a sympathetic ear and teacher's understanding whenever the writing process gets the better of me.

The publishers would like to thank the following for their thoughtful insights and perceptive comments during the development of the material:

Dalal Al Hitty, University of Bahrain, Bahrain; Karin Heuert Galvão, i-Study Interactive Learning, São Paulo, Brazil; Ohanes Sakris, Australian College of Kuwait, Kuwait; Eoin Jordan, Xi'an Jiaotong-Liverpool University, Suzhou, China; Aaron Rotsinger, Xi'an Jiaotong-Liverpool University, Suzhou, China; Dr. Osman Z. Barnawi, Royal Commission Yanbu Colleges & Institutes, Yanbu, Saudi Arabia; Andrew Lasher, SUNY Korea, Incheon, South Korea; Fatoş Uğur Eskiçirak, Bahçeşehir University, Istanbul, Turkey; Dr. Asmaa Awad, University of Sharjah, Sharjah, United Arab Emirates; Amy Holtby, The Petroleum Institute, Abu Dhabi, United Arab Emirates; Dr. Christina Gitsaki, Zayed University, Dubai, United Arab Emirates.

Printed and bound in Dubai

2022 2021 2020 2019 2018
10 9 8 7 6 5 4 3 2 1

PALGRAVE STUDY SKILLS

by bestselling author, **Stella Cottrell**

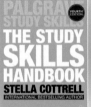  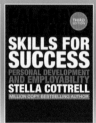

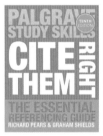 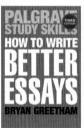 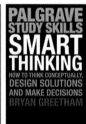   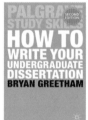

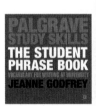 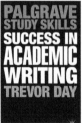  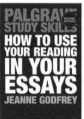 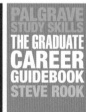 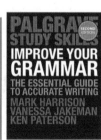